Praise for

BUSTED

"Equal parts serious journalism and sisterly sass, *Busted* is a personable and fast-reading ride. . . a shoe-leather journalistic procedural set against the ticking clock of the failing newspaper industry."

—New York Times Book Review

"The chick, noir version of *All the President's Men* with a little *Rocky*. . . and a little almost anything with Rosalind Russell or Barbara Stanwyck."

—Washington Post

"A riveting tale of two brave reporters who love what they do and are totally committed to doing what it takes to nail down their story. You've heard of police procedurals. This is a police-reporting procedural. Like the authors, the book is engaging, down to earth, and, at times, very funny. And it's an important testament to the power of journalism."

—USA Today

"*Busted* is a welcome addition to the literature of journalism procedurals."

"As investigative reporters for the *Philadelphia Daily News*, this writing duo won a Pulitzer Prize for their series on police corruption in Philadelphia. The story starts with Benny Martinez, a drug informant who walked into their newspaper offices and spilled some secrets. It ends by exposing the dirty dealings of an elite narcotics squad."

"A fast-paced, well-written true crime book."

"*Busted* is a very good book about very bad people, a great read about great injustice. . . . The hero here is journalism. . . the near-forgotten practice of walking the streets, paper and pad in hand, talking to people, and then writing about it. . . because there are stories that demand to be told. Ruderman and Laker told such a story, lifting out of obscurity the lives of others while imperiling their own. . . . *Busted* is proof that journalism still lives, still matters."

"A story that not only pounds at the door to come inside, but stands as a much-needed reminder that newspapers are and always have been and, as far as I know, always will be the bedrock of the art of journalism."

"*Busted: A Tale of Corruption and Betrayal in the City of Brotherly Love* is the scorching, devastating, and action-packed story of two journalists' journey into the dark heart of a major city. The obstacles they faced, the human tragedy they encountered, and their personal courage made me cry, cheer, and yearn for the newsroom. Wendy Ruderman and Barbara Laker are true heroes. . . . I love this book."

—Edna Buchanan, Pulitzer Prize–winning journalist and bestselling author

"I admire Wendy Ruderman and Barbara Laker, who are not only Pulitzer Prize–winning journalists, but fearless and fascinating women. *Busted* reads like a turbo-charged thriller, all the more compelling because it's true. Pick up a copy, and you won't be able to put it down."

—Lisa Scottoline

"*Busted* is a thoroughly engaging—who would have thought such a word could apply?—trip into Philadelphia's underworld, where cops prey on those they are pledged to protect. More than just an absorbing tale, Ruderman and Laker have written a reporter's procedural, one that ought to be read by anyone interested in the profession, and one that makes a compelling case for the essential importance of the work. Rich with character and incident, it's a complete original, and a love letter to newspapers in their hour of dire need."

—Mark Bowden, author of *Black Hawk Down*

"*Busted* is a taut, gritty story of drug dealers and corrupt cops written with passion, fury, and what Philadelphians refer to as attitude (pronounced 'atty-tood'). Ruderman and Laker have a lot of that, which is why they're two of the best reporters in the country."

—George Anastasia, author of *Blood and Honor* and *The Last Gangster*

"Prevailing against threats, intimidation, and the impending bankruptcy of their newspaper, Ruderman and Laker delivered a powerful series on police corruption, ultimately earning the Pulitzer Prize for investigative reporting. This is a gritty, true-life thriller about the intersection of policing, drug dealing, and news reporting."

—*Booklist* (starred review)

"Fans of *The Front Page* and *All the President's Men* will be transfixed by this astounding tale of police corruption. At the same time old-school tabloid reporters Ruderman and Laker are uncovering the story, their paper, the *Philadelphia Daily News*, is sinking—losing staff and other resources. But they persevere and end up not only with a great story but [also] a Pulitzer Prize."

—*New York Post*

"[A] gritty, honest, often surprisingly funny book."

—*Philadelphia Weekly*

"Part study in investigative journalism, it also delivers a commentary on the state of print journalism today, and justice."

—*New York Daily News*

"*Busted* is a Philadelphia classic. . . . It's an easy, breezy read but that's not to say it's insubstantial."

—*Philadelphia* magazine

"The authors . . . contextualize their process of unraveling a web of corrupt cops in an elite narcotics unit with events of tremendous change and upheaval in Philadelphia, its police department, the local newspaper business, and in their personal lives. . . . The book is a tough, lively lesson in how doing the right thing, the right way, may not be enough."

—*Publishers Weekly*

"The authors demonstrate the fearless tenacity of dedicated journalists who risk their personal health and safety to uncover the truth. In the process, they reveal their mastery in telling a good story by balancing the raw, shady elements with humor, suspense, and references to family life. Readers of true crime and students of sociology will especially enjoy this highly engaging read about the modern realities that plague many American cities."

—Library Journal

B USTED

WENDY RUDERMAN

BARBARA LAKER

A Tale of Corruption and Betrayal

BUSTED

in the City of Brotherly Love

HARPER

NEW YORK • LONDON • TORONTO • SYDNEY

HARPER

A hardcover edition of this book was published in 2014 by HarperCollins Publishers.

HarperCollins books may be purchased for educational, business, or sales promotional use. For information please e-mail the Special Markets Department at SPsales@harpercollins.com.

FIRST HARPER PAPERBACK EDITION PUBLISHED 2015.

Designed by Fritz Metsch

Library of Congress Cataloging-in-Publication Data has been applied for.

ISBN 978-0-06-208545-0 (pbk.)

15 16 17 18 19   OV/RRD   10 9 8 7 6 5 4 3 2 1

For my boys, Brody and Sawyer,
who give me immeasurable joy. I love you.

In memory of my father, Stan Ruderman, my spiritual guide.
Thank you for always cheering me on and for inspiring me to
dream—and dream big. In memory of my nephew, Jake, a little
firecracker who died too young.

—WENDY RUDERMAN

For my children, Josh and Anna,
who make everything in life better and brighter.
I'll never love anyone more.

In memory of my mom, Etta Laker, who gave me strength and
love. She taught me to never give up—and to take time to
dance in the kitchen.

—BARBARA LAKER

B USTED

1

VENTURA "BENNY" MARTINEZ HADN'T
SLEPT IN DAYS. THIS FRIGID DECEMBER
NIGHT, LIKE SO MANY OTHERS, HE SAT
AWAKE, STIFF-BACKED AND TENSE IN A
living room chair. His pudgy, sweaty fingers
gripped the handle of a .44 Ruger equipped
with an infrared laser to illuminate whoever
would be coming for him.

His wife, Sonia, and their two small children slept on a mattress in the dining room
behind him. There, they would be insulated
from any bullets that tore through the walls.

Benny locked his eyes on the front door
of his two-story brick Philadelphia row
house and waited. Maybe tonight he'd get
whacked. Maybe tomorrow. He didn't know
when. He just knew it would happen.

Even on those rare nights when he
could briefly doze off, slumped in a chair,
his chin hitting his chest, he'd bolt upright
in a cold sweat. He had a recurring nightmare in which Jeff Cujdik, the cop he had

worked for as a drug informant, blasted his face off with a shotgun.

Benny inched toward the living room windows. He split the plastic window blinds with his fingers and checked the front porch, then slowly moved his eyes up and down the block—over and over. A streetlight cast a dull, shadowy glow. No one was there. At least Benny couldn't spot anyone.

Benny stood stock-still.

"Babe, babe, what are you doing?" Sonia asked.

"Shhh," Benny whispered.

In the darkness, Benny listened to the sounds of the street: a far-off police siren, a dog's growl, a hip-hop pulse blaring from a car stereo, the buzz-saw whine of the El.

"I can't take this no more," Sonia said. "We've gotta leave up out of Philly."

"Nah. It will be okay," Benny told her. But Sonia knew Benny didn't believe his own words.

For three years, Benny had been happy and safe in this tan row house sandwiched into a narrow block of Pacific Street. It was a neighborhood where Latinos, blacks, and whites judged one another only by who went to work and who was on welfare.

Now he feared a silent sniper, maybe crouched behind a parked car or hidden in the shadow of a neighbor's porch.

Benny never thought it would come to this. Just a few months earlier, he'd considered Jeff a blood brother. Benny's kids called him Uncle Jeff.

They were an unlikely pair. Jeff, tall, muscular, and confident, with chiseled movie-star good looks, came from a family of cops; Benny, short, plump, and street-smart, was an ex–drug dealer. Yet they developed a bond, bitching about their wives, gushing over their kids. And they both got an adrenaline rush from danger.

Jeff was a narcotics cop who relied on Benny to bust drug dealers. Time and time again, Benny ticked off names for Jeff. He told Jeff what they sold, where they lived, and the places they stashed the drugs. Then Benny made drug buys, so Jeff could get a search warrant to raid the dealers' homes and make arrests. Benny was rewarded for each buy he made, and Jeff's arrest numbers skyrocketed. They stroked each other's egos. They rose together, mismatched allies, and both became stars of the game.

Benny was practically a lifer in the world of Philadelphia police informants. The tenure of the typical informant was short. Most ran out of people to roll on, and after they made lots of drug buys, dealers could figure out who had dimed them out. But Benny was the king. He had worked for Jeff for seven years. He was smooth and convincing, the perfect con man. Dealers believed Benny was part of their world because he had been for so long. That is, until something went terribly wrong.

Now Benny was convinced that Jeff wanted him dead. And maybe worse, so did Philly's drug dealers, who'd figured out Benny was a snitch. He had a target on his back. Too many people knew where to find him and how to gun him down.

Benny knew he couldn't live like this anymore.

He came up with a plan. Tomorrow was the day.

2

IT WAS A COLD BUT SUNNY DAY IN
EARLY DECEMBER 2008, AND MY WEEK-
DAY MORNING BEGAN IN A GROUND-
HOG DAY KIND OF WAY. AFTER I SLIPPED
into jeans, sweater, and sneakers for my job
as a reporter at the *Philadelphia Daily News*, I
served the kids Eggo waffles, submerged in
a lake of gooey syrup, on the black leather
couch. I turned on the TV. They always
complained when I turned on *Sesame Street*
or *Clifford the Big Red Dog,* so I put on *Sponge-
Bob*, or some other age-inappropriate cartoon, and went to fetch the newspaper.

We subscribed to both the *Philadelphia
Inquirer* and the *Daily News*, even though
I could get them for free at work. As fewer
and fewer people bought newspapers—let
alone had them delivered—I felt it was my
duty to support the dinosaur of an industry
that was mine. It was sad to me that ours was
the only house on the block to get a daily
newspaper. Seven days a week, a woman

drove up in a maroon minivan, rolled down the driver's-side window, and hurled the plastic-wrapped newspaper sleeve onto our front lawn, a grassy postage stamp dotted with weeds and bald patches. She barely slowed before banging a K-turn in the neighbor's driveway.

At 8:00 a.m., my husband, Karl, was still asleep. I had met Karl in a tae kwon do class back in the early 1990s. He was a second-degree black belt and taught classes three nights a week. I spent the entire class watching his firm butt as he demonstrated down block, center punch. I could see his navy-blue Fruit of the Loom briefs through his white uniform. He was lanky yet muscular, with a big, beaky nose, a sexy cleft chin, and doelike brown eyes that were so warm and gentle they caught me by surprise, and still do.

Most of the friction in our marriage centered on sleep—and who got more of it. At times, I resented that Karl could sleep in, but I told myself that he, as the stay-at-home parent, needed his sleep to handle Brody, five, and Sawyer, three. The boys had a way of pulling your nerves taut and snapping them over their little knees like kindling.

"Mom, I'm sticky. I need a wipe," Brody called from the couch.

"Okay." I kept reading the newspaper, over coffee, at the dining room table.

"Mommmm! I need a wipe!"

"Okay! Jesus! I'm coming!"

In my decade-long career as a reporter, I'd written stories that helped send a corrupt New Jersey state senator to jail, shamed a governor into firing a rotten state police superintendent, and prompted lawmakers to hold hearings on racial profiling by police, nearly jettisoning the career of an ambitious and powerful state attorney general. I'd earned my share of scalps. At work, I wasn't afraid to take on the law. At home, I was totally unable to lay down the law.

I had never put my kids in time-out. Not once. Not when Sawyer punched me in the back and barked, "Get me something to drink, little woman," or when he cleaned the television screen with a wet wipe and one of his many concoctions—a mixture of pancake syrup and body lotion.

I breast-fed Brody until he was two and a half. He'd walk up to me and say, "I want boob," and I'd lift my shirt and bring his curly blond head toward me. I couldn't say no. Ever.

If the kids wanted Popsicles for breakfast, fine. Though every so often, I got tough: "No Popsicle until you finish that whole bowl of Apple Jacks." Then I'd add, "I mean it."

If they wanted dinner in the bathtub, I spoon-fed them spaghetti while they played with a fleet of blue and yellow plastic boats. Chunks of tomato and strands of pasta drifted to the bottom of the sudsy water and left an oily slick on the white porcelain.

I allowed them to watch so much TV that they went around the house singing jingles to commercials for Nationwide insurance and electric wheelchairs for the elderly—"I want to go, Go, GO in my Hoveround."

When Brody woke up in the middle of the night and stumbled into our bedroom on his stick-figure legs, I held up the covers and nestled him close, even though I knew he kept Karl awake. Brody flopped around all night, kicking and jabbing Karl with his little toenails, until Karl fled to Brody's bed or squeezed into bed with Sawyer and his menagerie of stuffed animals. Karl was a nighttime nomad, condemned to wander the Land of Bad Parenting.

Karl liked to say that I was a great mom and a terrible parent. Part of it was guilt. A workaholic, I was never home during the week. The other part was fear. The responsibility of being a parent intimidated me. So I handed over the job to Karl. He stayed home with the kids while I went off to work and sank my teeth into the hide of some crooked or incompetent city official. This way, if the kids refused to eat veggies, if they were disrespectful to other adults, if they didn't do their homework, if they became social outcasts and landed in therapy, I could blame Karl.

Karl was good at the job, too. He had the mommy thing down. He was loving and stern all at once. Of course, I didn't help much. When Karl went out grocery shopping or to the store, chaos and mischief ruled. I became the third kid. On summer nights, I allowed Brody and Sawyer to catch fireflies in Tupperware containers and let them free in the house. We turned off the lights and watched them flit around the ceiling, giggling. Sawyer sometimes dumped entire bottles of bubble bath into the tub. He then jumped out of the water and did body slides across the hardwood floors in our living room. I quickly cleaned up the snail-trail of suds with a towel before Karl came home. Karl was annoyingly compulsive about water on the hardwood. In the mornings before work, I let them play with mounds of moldable Moon Sand at the dining room table or allow them to decorate the chairs with Lightning McQueen stickers. Or they turned our kitchen into a bowling alley, flinging ripe peaches into V-shaped lines of Dixie cups. The game left splats of sticky peach juice all over the tile floor. Then I scooted out the door, leaving Karl to mop up the mess and deal with two kids, hopped up on sugar, smacking each other with pillows and wrestling naked.

It took me less than ten minutes to get from my New Jersey house to the foot of the Ben Franklin Bridge. From there, it was a straight shot down the Vine Street Expressway, through Chinatown, to Broad Street, the city's north-south artery. Broad Street cut through Philadelphia, spilling down and around City Hall like an asphalt stream.

The *Daily News* was a white multitiered building that resembled a giant wedding cake topped with a clock tower and brass dome. We had shared 400 North Broad with the *Philadelphia Inquirer*, or *Inky*, since 1957, when *Inky* owner Walter Annenberg purchased the scrappy but near-bankrupt tabloid, but locals still referred to the eighteen-floor landmark as the Inquirer Building. The *Daily News* was the *Inquirer*'s brassy little sister with flaming red hair and an attitude. The edifice stood alone on Broad Street, cut off from the city's other skyscrapers by the expressway. Inga Saffron, the *Inquirer*'s acclaimed architecture critic, liked to say that the building's location was symbolic of an independent press, an unbiased government watchdog, "the noble, lone seeker of truth."

Around midafternoon, Benny walked through the front doors. He stood in the front lobby and reached into his jacket pocket to pull out a crumpled piece of paper with my name scrawled on it.

"I'm here to speak to Wendy Rudumam," Benny said, butchering my last name. The security guard nodded and dialed my extension.

That morning, Benny had put his plan to get help and protection in motion. He had gone to the Police Advisory Commission, a watchdog over the 6,600-member city police force. Benny talked to Wellington Stubbs, whose job was to investigate citizen complaints against police officers. The commission was supposed to be independent from the police department and the mayor's office, but it relied on city funding. It was so understaffed and underfunded that Wellington and a handful of other investigators struggled to keep up with complaints. The commission lacked the clout and resources to do much about rogue officers. Police corruption in Philly was like a recurring cancer that reared its ugly head every ten years or so, and the commission could do little to stop or expose it. This frustrated Wellington. So he fed me story tips.

Wellington called to let me know that he was sending Benny over. Although Wellington didn't feel like he could immediately help Benny, he felt urgency. Benny didn't come across like your run-of-the-mill disgruntled criminal who wanted to seek revenge on a cop and sue the city for money. In words and actions, Benny sounded and looked desperate. Wellington didn't give me any details about Benny's story. He just figured maybe I could help him and told me so—a decision that would later cost him his job.

I headed to the lobby. Odds were, this would be a waste of time. Most stories about police corruption or brutality were garbage. They often came from lowlifes who wanted either to have their criminal records wiped clean or a payout from city coffers. Or from people who had no proof, nothing to back up their story. But some stories were the real deal. I prided myself on knowing the difference. The fact that Benny came to me through Wellington would give his tale extra weight.

Benny and I greeted each other warily. We shook hands. His palm felt moist and meaty. Benny had the baleful look of a tired basset hound, a round face atop a short, plump body. His brown eyes sat afloat in bloodshot pools of white. He wore dark blue Dickies work pants and a puffy charcoal-gray jacket, embroidered with BENNY and GEGNAS CHRYSLER JEEP, the auto dealership where he cleaned and buffed cars.

I led him up the lobby's worn marble steps near the elevators. The lobby was a tomb of marble and gold-painted molding. The light fixture was a giant globe with blue oceans and white continents encircled by a brass Saturn-like ring. The *Inquirer* used to cover the world, but the paper had called home its reporters and shuttered its last foreign bureau, an outpost in Jerusalem, in 2006. The *Daily News* had never covered the world. It covered Philly. Period.

The ornate lobby was the magisterial curtain that hid the building's grimy—and desolate—innards. Brian Tierney, the new CEO and head of an investors group that purchased the *Inky* and *Daily News* in June 2006, now hoped to sell the building. The investors needed the cash. Layoffs and financial cutbacks had left the place half empty. The printing presses had been moved to a plant in the suburbs more than a decade ago. The building was so empty that randy staffers roamed its vacant floors looking for rooms where they could have sex.

I'd come to the *Daily News* about two years ago as an *Inquirer* refugee. After four years as an *Inquirer* reporter, I jumped ship and landed on the *Daily News* dinghy to avoid being laid off. At the time, I was one of some seventy *Inquirer* newsroom staffers on the chopping block. For the *Daily News*, this was an era of buttercream-frosted sheet cakes served at newsroom good-byes. So many staffers had taken buyouts that the *Daily News* was exempt from this round of cuts.

I led Benny through the lobby, then he followed me down a flight of steps that led to the *Daily News*. I heard the clack of Benny's industrial work boots on the tile floor, where a black, gooey gunk made its home in the crevices. The ceiling was all exposed water pipes and wires. A neon 1950s-style sign mounted outside the newsroom read "Philadelphia *Daily News*. The People Paper." I pushed opened the beige door to reveal a football field of empty desks separated by chest-high gray partitions. Fluorescent lights hung from the ceiling like suspended tanning beds. A stout metal filing cabinet doubled as a table, with a fax machine on each end. We walked past stacks of yellowed newspapers, dusty dictionaries, a broken typewriter, and an ancient unplugged TV set.

We sat down in the "penalty box," the reporters' nickname for the small meeting area enclosed by low glass walls, slightly bigger than the time-out box for hockey players.

"Do you want coffee? Or water?" I asked.

I hoped he'd say no. I wasn't sure we had cups, let alone fresh coffee.

"Nah. I'm OK."

Benny sat across from me, his hands folded on the table. He licked his lips, ran his tongue over a chipped top tooth, and began talking, his words a whispered cascade. I leaned in. I opened my reporter's notepad and started to scribble: "Ventura Martinez Perez. Confidential Informant. Jeffrey Cujdik, cop, Narcotics Field Unit."

Over the next forty-five minutes, Benny laid out a Shakespearean tale of trust, betrayal, and revenge. I felt stressed and overwhelmed, not certain how to proceed, but my gut told me there was something to his story.

"Benny, can you excuse me for a minute? I'll be right back."

Barbara Laker was at her desk. Of all the reporters in the room, she was the one I admired most. Like me, she lived the job. She'd been a reporter since 1979 and worked at the *Daily News* for more than sixteen years. When I came to the *Daily News*, she was my editor. At the time, her kids were away in college, she was mourning the dissolution of a twenty-five-year marriage, and she thought the editing gig might fill a void. Instead, it gave her migraines. During her three-year editing stint, she nurtured cub reporters so much that they pegged her "Mama Laker." She was known for baking gooey chocolate brownies for staff parties and mentoring rookies, helping them craft their stories.

Barbara walked them through how to master street reporting, sometimes even writing out questions for them. She knew she did too much hand-holding, but she wanted the best story possible and enjoyed seeing inexperienced reporters learn and get better. But as time went on, she grew frustrated with reporters who returned to the office with little in their notebooks. She couldn't understand how some reporters were satisfied with canned interviews that everyone else had. How could you be a reporter without any fire in your belly? Barbara wondered. She had to resist the urge to push them out of the way and just do the job herself.

Barbara was a sweetheart who, unlike me, never dropped the f-bomb or got crass about her sex life. Barbara was like no boss I'd had at the *Inquirer*. *Inquirer* editors came across as Ivy League intellectuals—cynical, self-important, stiff. The men resembled aging college professors, with disheveled, thinning hair, khaki pants, striped ties, and light blue or white dress shirts, usually with the sleeves rolled up. The women looked more like aging Flower Power hippies, with long flowing skirts, Birkenstock sandals, no makeup, and flat, graying hair that hadn't seen a box of Clairol in years. So when I first laid eyes on Barbara, I thought, Who is this bimbo?

Barbara was oblivious to her ability to make men's heads turn, even at our workplace cafeteria, where a horny *Inquirer* reporter once had the chutzpah to ask me if her boobs were real. At fifty, she was an avid runner, trim and shapely, with three marathons under her belt.

Barbara had long, wavy highlighted blond hair and a tangerine slice of a nose. Her big green eyes, flecked with caramel, reminded me of top-of-the-line granite kitchen counters.

She rimmed them with dark olive eyeliner and a hint of gray-ish blue eye shadow. With her coral lip gloss, silver hoop ear-rings, snug skirts, and candy-colored blouses, Barbara came off all bubble-gum—wifty and gee-whiz. But that was just her facade. She was a master at getting people to talk, using her charm, smarts, and girlish warmth to get into houses and get the story. She truly got people. She knew just what to say to convince anyone from criminal to victim that she was friend, not foe, and that they could let their guard down, she could be trusted. When she stood to leave with her full notebook, they would invariably say, "I can't believe I told you all this! I haven't told anyone."

Obsessive reporters often describe themselves with one phrase: "Journalism is in my blood." And Barbara and I had the same blood.

I grew up in a family of newspaper readers. A newspaper landed on my front porch every morning. Each week, a de-livery boy showed up at my door for his $3.50. At night, I'd walk by my parents' bedroom and see them lying beside one another, each of their faces obscured by newsprint stretched between their hands. My parents loved newspapers. When I got busted in college for underage drinking and my arrest got written up in the local paper, my parents cut out the arti-cle and saved it in a scrapbook. They were thrilled to see my name in the paper, even for something criminal.

My dad, who grew up in Brooklyn and was short and bald-ing, spent his entire career as an accountant for a car dealer-ship. He dreamed of bigger things for himself and for me, my sister, and my brother. He took us as kids to Broadway shows, read us poems by A. E. Housman and Edwin Arlington Rob-inson, and recited—from memory—Ernest Thayer's "Casey at the Bat" from the top of the three steps leading from our kitchen to the living room. He took us to great restaurants every Friday night. "Eat slow. Eat slow," he'd tell us, wanting us to savor the meal. He planned family vacations to historic landmarks, like Colonial Williamsburg, where we complained of boredom while watching actors in eighteenth-century costume churn butter in the scorching August heat.

My dad, who died of cancer when I was twenty-eight, thought I was a superstar. He believed I could do anything and do it better than anyone else. When I graduated from Columbia University with a master's in journalism, he wanted to know why some other student—and not me—got an award at graduation: Didn't the professors recognize how great I was? A lot of my ambition as a reporter was tied to my need to live up to my father's galactic expectations.

Barbara came of age in journalism's heyday. With a gaggle of other teenage know-it-all Baby Boomer idealists, she decided she wanted to be a reporter in the 1970s when Watergate broke. She was fascinated by *Washington Post* reporters Bob Woodward and Carl Bernstein, and how they, with the help of a then-mysterious source known only as Deep Throat, uncovered the most notorious political scandal in American history.

She wanted to know step by step how Woodward and Bernstein had unearthed a trove of secrets, including sabotage, spying, and bribery, that in the end would topple a president. She still remembered huddling around the boxy black-and-white TV with her family to hear Richard Nixon resign in August 1974.

That year, applications to journalism schools reached an all-time high. Barbara's was among them. Since then, two of the five newspapers that Barbara worked for—the *Clearwater Sun* and the *Dallas Times-Herald*—have died. A third, the *Seattle Post-Intelligencer*, is now online only.

The afternoon when I first met Benny, I hoped that Barbara wanted in on his story. Truth be told, I was tired of being alone in the trenches battling police misdeeds. I'd already gained a reputation as the go-to reporter for people who had run-ins with cops. I'd written stories about a cop caught with a racist sticker in his locker, a cop who unleashed a testosterone-fueled beating on a group of women at a baby shower, and a swarm of cops who stomped on and kicked the heads of three shooting suspects while a TV news helicopter filmed overhead. I was sick of being called a "cop hater" and a "bitch" by anonymous callers. I needed reinforcements, someone to help steel up my backbone, an ally in the fight.

3

BARBARA JOINED US IN THE PENALTY BOX, AND BENNY STARTED FROM THE TOP. HE'D BEGUN WORKING WITH JEFF CUJDIK IN LATE 2001, AFTER JEFF caught him selling marijuana on a corner. Benny was thirty-five years old and on probation for a prior drug conviction. He didn't want to go to prison, so he accepted Jeff's offer to turn informant.

"I knew I was gonna do some time," Benny told us. "So I said, 'Well, I gotta do what I gotta do.' "

So Benny became Confidential Informant 103. Roughly three times a week, Jeff picked up Benny in an unmarked police car. They worked a list of suspected drug homes. Benny's job was to knock on the door and make a drug buy, while Jeff and his partner watched from a hidden location. Benny used cash that Jeff had given him, called prerecorded buy money, for the drugs. Benny then handed over the drug packets to Jeff, who put them into evidence.

Once the deal was done, Jeff prepared an application for a search warrant, which he would need to enter a home. In the warrant, he typically included why he was targeting a certain house, what drugs he saw Informant 103 buy, where he bought them, and from whom. Sometimes Jeff had a first and last name of the suspect; other times only a physical description and a street name like "Macho" or "Blackie."

A judge then issued a search warrant that Jeff would use when he and his squad members busted into the house.

The police department, through Jeff, paid Benny cash for the jobs. He usually got $20 for each drug buy and $150 to $250 for a big drug seizure, and if police found weapons, the department paid Benny an additional $100 for each gun. And Jeff nearly doubled his $55,400 salary in court overtime because each time he locked up a dealer, he had to testify in the case. More important, Jeff got attaboys from the "white shirts," sergeants and captains who had earned enough stripes to hang up their uniform blues.

Over the years, Benny emerged as one of the city's most prolific drug informants, and Jeff became one of the department's golden boys, a favorite son who brought home the stats and made his bosses look good. Jeff, perhaps more than other cops, needed informants like Benny. With his clean-cut looks and his I-own-this-town swagger, Jeff's appearance screamed cop. No dealer would be stupid enough to sell to him.

Benny told us that at first he and Jeff did things by the book, but then the lies began. If Benny couldn't score drugs from a house, Jeff sometimes told him to buy elsewhere. Then in the application for a search warrant, Jeff would say that the drugs came from the targeted house. Benny even set up some of his closest friends—people he considered family, people who trusted and loved him. But that wasn't the only secret Benny and Jeff shared.

About four years after they started working together, Jeff rented a house he had purchased for $30,000 to Benny and his family. The rent was $300 a month—a steal in Philly's rental market.

Some of the cash that Benny earned as a police informant flowed back to Jeff in the form of rent money. This was against police department rules, and Jeff knew he'd get in big trouble if internal affairs found out.

The beginning of the end of their friendship came in 2006, though Jeff and Benny didn't know it at the time. In November of that year, Benny tipped Jeff off to a drug dealer named Raul Nieves. Benny knew Raul from an auto-detailing shop where he had worked. Raul knew Benny as Benny Blanco, a reference to a character in the 1993 movie *Carlito's Way*. In the film, Al Pacino plays a Puerto Rican ex–drug dealer dogged by Benny Blanco, a pesky young gangster from the Bronx.

Benny got Raul's cell number and arranged to buy $125 worth of weed, enough to roll about fifty joints. After that, Benny hounded Raul for more pot, but Raul brushed him off. Something didn't feel right.

Jeff and his squad later tore apart Raul's Ford Expedition and found fifty-six orange-tinted crack baggies stashed behind the dashboard. Another twenty baggies were hidden behind a driver's-side door panel. They locked up Raul on felony drug charges.

Raul hired a meticulous, serious-minded veteran defense attorney named Stephen Patrizio. Right away, Raul suspected that Confidential Informant 103 was Benny. Patrizio hired a private investigator to tail Benny home from work.

Raul's case lingered in criminal court. Again and again,

hearing dates got scheduled, then postponed. Raul waited, coolly. Finally, on October 10, 2008—almost two years after Benny bought weed from Raul and two months before Benny came to the *Daily News*—the case leaped forward, exploding at Jeff's feet.

Jeff sat in the witness stand. Patrizio stood before him. He was short and stocky, with a fuzz of hair on a mostly bald head, his pants pulled up perhaps a bit too high, and belted over his paunch. Those who wrote him off as a mild-mannered, harmless geek would soon be proven wrong.

Patrizio took out a copy of Police Directive 15, the rules that officers should follow when dealing with informants, and showed it to Jeff.

Patrizio began to read aloud: " 'Police personnel will maintain professional objectivity in dealing with informants. No personal relationships will jeopardize the objectivity of the informant or the integrity of the department.' "

Patrizio paused and looked up at Jeff. "Correct?"

"Correct," Jeff replied.

Then Patrizio pounced. He stuck a photo under Jeff's nose. It was a snapshot of Benny walking out of Jeff's house.

"Without asking you anything about the person depicted in the picture, do you recognize that street?"

"Yes," Jeff said.

"And not only do you recognize the street, but you recognize the house that the informant is coming out of, correct?"

"I don't know exactly what house the individual came out of, but I can identify one house on that block," Jeff said.

"You can identify the house of 1939 East Pacific Street?"

"I own that house," Jeff said.

"That was my question. You can identify that house?"

"I answered the question," Jeff said, icily.

Patrizio told the judge that he planned to subpoena Informant 103. Defense attorneys often filed motions seeking to drag informants into court. Ninety-nine percent of the time, prosecutors and judges laugh at the request. Confidential informants were just that—confidential. For good reason. Judges protected their identity to prevent drug dealers from killing them. But this case was different. Raul already knew Benny's identity, and he hadn't touched him.

"He has known who he is for long periods of time, and nothing has happened to him," Patrizio argued.

The judge saw Patrizio's point, and the court issued a subpoena for "Benny Blanco," aka "Benny Martinez."

Jeff panicked. With their relationship exposed, he moved to cut all ties with Benny. Jeff put the rental property up for sale and told Benny that he had to leave. Benny wouldn't budge.

So in December 2008, Jeff filed a complaint in landlord-tenant court to evict Benny and Sonia, noting that he'd received no rent since October. Jeff then deactivated Benny as an informant.

By the time Benny came to Barbara and me, he was desperate. Benny, the woman he referred to as his wife, Sonia, and their two small children had nowhere to go.

He sat across from us, seemingly terrified, convinced that he'd soon be a dead man. Word had spread on the street that Benny was a snitch. He feared Raul wanted to kill him. If not Raul, some other drug dealer. He told us that he'd opened his door to find a chunk of cheese on the stoop. It was a street message: Benny was a rat.

He told us that, like prisoners, he, Sonia, and the kids spent nights in the upstairs middle bedroom, where his ten-month-old daughter Gianni slept. He pushed her crib against the wall and dragged a king-size mattress onto the pink carpet. He told his three-year-old son Giovanni to pretend they were camping. He figured they were safer there, holed away in a Benny-made bunker. But he still couldn't sleep. He sat saucer-eyed, fixated on the bedroom door, convinced the knob would turn and he'd see the barrel of a gun.

Jeff no longer had his back. In fact, Benny told us he feared him, that Jeff could patiently lie in wait for the perfect moment to put a bullet in his head, which we later learned was Benny being overdramatic.

"I was dreaming the other night that Jeff shot me in my face," Benny said. "Jeff is a hunter. He likes to hunt. . . . I could be sitting on my porch smoking a cigarette and I could get shot real easily."

Benny stopped talking. Barbara and I looked at each other. We sat back in our chairs. Quiet. Dubious.

"Look, it's true. I could call Jeff right now," Benny said.

Benny flipped open his cell. Jeff answered immediately. Barbara and I practically laid our upper bodies across the table. I kneeled on my chair seat, propped myself up on my elbows, and shoved my head next to Benny's cell phone. I was close enough to kiss his cheek. I could see every follicle of his scant pencil mustache and goatee and smell his cologne. Barbara did the same on the other side.

"You know I know a lot," Benny was saying.

"I don't know what you're talking about," Jeff said.

Benny tried to bait him, but Jeff gave up nothing. "Don't do anything stupid," he warned Benny.

The conversation was short, and Jeff sounded guarded, edgy. Could Jeff really kill Benny or find some street thug to do it for him? We didn't know. What we did know was that Jeff wanted Benny out of his life.

Before long, I'd want the same thing.

4

BENNY WAS ALL ABOUT BENNY, AND HE KNEW HOW TO PLAY PEOPLE TO GET WHAT HE WANTED. AFTER COPS BUSTED HIM FOR SELLING COCAINE IN 1994, Benny summoned tears during his sentencing hearing. He told the judge that he started dealing only because he had no money to buy a birthday present for a daughter from his first marriage, that jobs and opportunities were scarce in the hood, especially for a high school dropout like him. Sure, he knew it was wrong, but the drug trade was all there was, often the only means of survival in Philly's tar pit of hopelessness and poverty. Benny's wife and kids, who sat behind him in the courtroom, began to sob, and the judge cut him a break, meting out house arrest instead of prison time.

"I had the whole courtroom in tears," Benny boasted. "People came up to me afterwards and said, 'Good luck to you.'"

When Benny needed money to buy cocaine and crack, he concocted tales of personal tragedy so people would feel sorry for him and not be able to say no. He'd knock on doors of family friends and frantically recount how his wife, his father-in-law, whomever, had been in a serious car accident and he needed cash to get a cab to the hospital or to get the banged-up car out of the impound lot. He once weaseled money out of his oldest son's high school friends by telling them that his son had been injured in a car wreck. The friends were shocked to see Benny Jr.—unscathed—at school the next day.

One day Benny showed up at the bodega that his oldest daughter managed with a tale of woe. He mumbled, through half-paralyzed lips, cradling a limp arm, that he'd suffered a stroke.

Another time, he told me that he felt weak and was bleeding profusely from his rectum. A few days later, he told me he had colon cancer and needed chemotherapy but didn't have health insurance. Then he said doctors feared that the cancer had spread to his vocal cords because his voice sounded raspy. When I went to the store and told Benny's daughter about his cancer, she looked at me and said, "Yeah, he told me the same thing. I'm waiting to see paperwork."

Of course Barbara and I didn't realize that Benny was still a drug addict, who often told lies to feed his habit, until long after he first came to the *Daily News*. He told us that he had given up drugs years ago and wanted to be an informant to make things right and clean up the hood.

He was convincing. He was good, real good.

Benny was instantly likable. There was something about him—people always wanted to help him; they wanted to trust him. He cracked jokes at his own expense and was an expert on salsa music. Pick any song and Benny could name the artist, the producer, and the label. He saw himself as a tough guy, but actually he was mushy at the core, quick to tear up and say he loved you—"Youse like family," he'd say. He was a hard worker, known as one of the best auto detailers in Philadelphia. He won trophies in detailing competitions and specialized in exotics—Beamers, Mercedes, Escalades—the cars of drug dealers. He could hand-polish black cars without leaving a single swirl. Even after Benny stole chrome tire rims worth $2,200 from an auto-detail shop, the owner told Barbara that he liked Benny and would hire him back. Another shop owner swindled by Benny told me that he still loved Benny and would "cry at his funeral." Again and again, people told us that Benny had a good heart, but drugs made him do evil things.

Jeff, too, fell under his spell. Jeff, a decorated and seasoned cop who regularly dealt with some of Philly's seediest characters, let his guard down with Benny. He allowed Benny into his life and routinely helped him out. When Benny told Jeff that he needed money for child support, Jeff gave him the cash. When Benny said he was stressed out, Jeff gave him money for a trip to the Jersey Shore. When Benny needed a job, Jeff got him a gig working for a cop friend who owned an air-duct cleaning business.

And when Benny needed a place to live, Jeff told him that he could help him out. Jeff told Benny that he owned a house on Pacific Street, and Benny could rent it from him. This was something Barbara and I were able to confirm. We found court documents showing that Jeff did in fact own the house. And Benny gave us a copy of the rental agreement and other paperwork showing that Benny and Sonia lived there and paid rent to Jeff. This was just one part of Benny's story that checked out. The thing about Benny was, buried underneath his lies, there was truth.

Truth that Barbara and I would prove.

Benny told us that because Jeff had moved to evict Benny, both of them would show up at landlord-tenant court for a hearing before a judge. As the plaintiff, Jeff was expected to tell the judge that Benny had failed to pay rent, and he wanted him out.

Barbara and I knew one of us had to show up in court to see Jeff and witness the showdown between the two men. Benny assured us that Sonia would be there, too, so Barbara went to the house they had rented from Jeff to meet her a few days before the court hearing.

Sonia greeted Barbara warmly, but she was visibly scared; she knew Benny was terrified. Sonia was not the shy or skittish type. She was a tough ghetto girl who grew up in the bloody Badlands, an embattled section of Philly held hostage by gun-packing drug dealers who lorded over corners.

Sonia favored fake nails, long as daggers. She painted them hot pink or blood red. Her chubby body was inked with tattoos. One on her forearm read "Angel," a tribute to her first son, a stillborn. Two days before her due date, the doctor couldn't find a heartbeat. The umbilical cord had gotten tangled around Angel's neck. Sonia, then only twenty years old, chose to give birth to him without an epidural or sedatives. She wanted to feel Angel come into this world.

Sonia wasn't afraid to feel or fight. Not girlie fighting, with hair pulling and clawing at her opponent, but full-throttle punches. She went straight for the face. She could lock it up. Benny liked that about Sonia.

The day of the hearing, set to begin at 8:45 a.m., Barbara walked in the thirty-five-degree chill to municipal court on Eleventh Street in the shadow of City Hall. Her heart was pounding. She went through security, turned off her cell, and took the elevator to the fourth floor.

A court clerk approached. "Ma'am, are you a landlord?"

"No," Barbara answered.

"Are you a tenant?"

"No."

Barbara wanted to give as little information as possible.

"Then who are you?"

Barbara knew she couldn't lie. "I'm a reporter for the *Daily News*," she replied.

"Well, you can't be here," she said.

"Yes, I can," she said, trying to sound authoritative, not belligerent. "It's open court. It's not closed to the media." Barbara showed the clerk her business card.

The clerk ushered Barbara into an adjoining room. Barbara was panicked. She couldn't miss this hearing. She explained as politely as possible that she was allowed to observe the court proceedings.

"I'll be back," the clerk said, looking Barbara up and down, probably wondering why she seemed so desperate about a landlord-tenant dispute.

Barbara waited, tapping her foot nervously and twirling her hair. Finally, after about ten minutes, the clerk returned.

"Okay. I checked. You can go in," the clerk said. "Just no tape recorder."

"Thank you," Barbara said. "No tape. I promise."

When Jeff sauntered into the landlord-tenant courtroom, he had no idea that Barbara was seated, watching. Jeff plopped down next to his attorney near the front. He looked straight ahead and appeared calm as he propped his right ankle on top of his left knee.

Benny and Sonia took seats far from Barbara, on the other side of the room. Barbara glanced over at Benny. His face and ears were beet-red.

He leaned over and whispered in Sonia's ear: "Jeff thinks he's Mr. Big Shot. I wanna get up and smack him."

"Calm down," Sonia said, patting him on the knee.

Judge Bradley Moss called Jeff's case, and Sonia and Benny approached the witness table. Moss pointed out that Benny and Sonia hadn't paid rent for three months. Benny tried to explain that he'd stopped paying rent when Jeff put the house up for sale, but Moss, who couldn't understand why that mattered, started to calculate how much they owed Jeff in rent and attorney fees.

"May I say something?" Benny asked.

"Absolutely," Moss said.

"The reason my lease was never renewed was because me and him are real good friends, all right. We are real good friends. Every time I paid him, he never gave me rent receipts because we were good friends. . . . Until the beginning of October, then I went through a little something with him because I worked for him as a CI. I'm his CI. Okay. I'm living in his property."

Benny's voice started to shake. "I had a defendant named Raul Nieves," he began. "When I told Jeff I had the subpoena right here, he automatically wanted me out of the house. That's the reason why I'm here today. And I don't think it's right that after I put a lot of people away and took guns off the street, I'm getting treated like this. My life is in danger right now, and no one is helping me."

"Well, that's a different issue," Moss began.

Benny's voice became shrill. "Right now they are looking for me to kill me and my family and nobody is there to help me. And he's supposed to be a good friend, Jeff!"

He turned sideways to look at Jeff. But Jeff looked stone-faced, his eyes fixed on Moss.

"You were a good friend to me, man. I do anything," Benny quavered.

Benny was on the verge of tears. It seemed as if every time Barbara and I saw Benny, he cried, spigot-like.

"Sheriff! Sheriff! Sir, you're in a court of law," said Moss, summoning backup, sensing that things could turn ugly or, worse yet, explosive.

"I'm getting treated . . . ," Benny said, his voice trailing off.

"You are in a court of law. I'm not Judge Judy. This is a real court," Moss said sternly.

Benny apologized. Moss told him to address him, not Jeff.

Benny hung his head. He wiped his eyes and cheeks with his palms.

"We'll take a break," Moss said.

"Can I use your bathroom?" Benny asked, sounding like a little kid.

Benny and Sonia looked beaten down as they walked to the hallway. Barbara saw Sonia slip into the ladies' room and followed her in.

"Benny's doin' bad. I hate to see him like this," Sonia whispered, leaning against the sink.

Sonia and Benny went way back. She'd fallen for him in the late 1990s. She was just seventeen when she saw him hanging on the corner of Howard and Cambria, the heart of Philly's open-air drug market. She was walking to the corner store, a half block from the row house where she lived with her mom.

"You have nice hair," she told him in her coarse, seductive way. He smiled impishly and slowly stroked his right hand over coarse black hair that he swept back and gelled to a sticky sheen.

Back then, Benny was thirty-four and living with Susette, his first love and mother of his three children. But Benny was smitten with Sonia, and he'd run around on Susette before. Benny was thick and chunky, yet saw himself as a sculpted stud. He said that he would have started messing around with Sonia that day, only she was too young. Never mind that he was with Susette.

Then one night, Benny went to a bar alone and ran into Sonia. He couldn't help but notice her. She was in the middle of one of her vicious all-out cat fights. Some woman had made her mad, and Sonia went off, going for the woman's hair and earrings.

"I gripped her up because I had to break up the fight," Benny told us. "She was like, 'Get the fuck off.' I was like, 'Yo. It's me.' She couldn't believe it. I dragged her outside. From then on, we just started messing around," Benny recalled.

The romance began. Susette found out and told Benny she was done with him once and for all.

Barbara and I often wondered why Sonia stuck by Benny, putting up with all his drama and bullshit. Benny once pulled his shirt collar down in the newsroom to show us a tattoo on the left side of his chest. The tattoo was of a heart with the name "Sue" for Susette in the middle. He refused to remove it. "She's my first love," he'd tell Sonia. Benny called Susette his wife; he called Sonia his wife. He never married either. Now, convinced that he was going to get popped in the head, mob-style, he persuaded Sonia to stick with him, that they were a team.

Sonia stood in the court bathroom and dried her hands, over and over, until the paper towel fell apart.

"When he gets out the car, I always be watching him," she told Barbara. "He knows all these people out to kill him."

Barbara told Sonia to go ahead of her back into the courtroom so nobody saw them together.

Moss gave Benny time to compose himself, then tried to keep him on point. Moss explained that Benny and Sonia owed $1,200 in unpaid rent, $350 in attorney's fees, and $62 in court costs. If they paid up, they could stay for twenty-one days. After that, Jeff could kick them out.

Benny said he understood. Moss asked a clerk if the sheriff was around.

"I don't want any problems in the elevator, so I don't care who leaves first. But I want the other party, the other side, to sit in the courtroom for five, ten minutes so that we don't have any problems in the elevator or outside, okay?" Moss asked.

"Okay. No problem," Benny said.

Benny volunteered to leave first. Barbara hung back as he and Sonia left the courtroom, then she followed Jeff to the elevator.

"Hi, Officer Cujdik," she said, holding out her hand. "I'm Barbara Laker, a reporter for the *Daily News*, and I just wanted to ask you a few questions."

Jeff looked puzzled but smiled and shook her hand. "About what?"

He wore blue jeans, brown work boots, and a blue T-shirt under a black North Face sweatshirt. At thirty-five, Jeff Cujdik (pronounced Chud-ick) stood six-foot-two with an athletic build, broad shoulders, and piercing blue eyes. His thick brown hair was neatly moussed into rows of tiny spikes. Jeff was practically groomed to be a cop. He grew up in the city's northeast section, a mostly safe white working-class neighborhood—Philly's version of Cop Land. Jeff's dad, Louis Cujdik, was a near-legendary narcotics officer, a cop's cop who mentored rookies. Drug dealers knew him by name, and some feared him. His older brother, Richard, was also a cop, married to a city assistant district attorney.

Jeff's younger brother, Gregory, was the splinter in this family of wooden lawmen. Gregory was twenty-nine when he pleaded guilty to felony drug charges after he sold pot to an undercover cop in a suburban town far from Philly.

Jeff graduated from an all-boys Catholic high school, where he wasn't a standout among his 215 classmates. He didn't participate in a single club or sport, and few classmates, even those who had sat near him in homeroom, could remember much about him. After graduation in 1992, Jeff got a job in maintenance for the Southeastern Pennsylvania Transportation Authority, or SEPTA, the city's rail and bus system. He married Jeanette, an attractive and kindhearted woman who'd graduated from an all-girls Catholic high school and stayed at home with their two young daughters.

Jeff joined the police force in 1997 and quickly landed a coveted spot on the narcotics field unit, where plainclothes officers cultivated tips on drug houses and used informants to bust them. Jeff's dad and brother also worked in the same unit.

Based on how Benny had described Jeff to us, Barbara thought he would look cold, be dismissive, and have an edge, an attitude. He wasn't at all what Barbara expected. He seemed approachable, with no hint of a don't-you-dare-come-near-me look.

When Barbara introduced herself to Jeff near the elevator, he didn't dismiss her curtly. Instead Jeff was polite, almost soft-spoken.

Barbara asked him about renting his house to an informant.

Jeff didn't hesitate to answer. "I'm Jeff Cujdik, the landlord," he said calmly. "I'm not here as a police officer." He knew that it would be a mistake to tell Barbara that he, as an officer, was collecting rent from his informant.

So he had to tell Barbara that he, like any other landlord, was renting a house to Benny and his family, and he was trying to evict them because they hadn't paid rent. Nothing more.

Barbara asked him for his phone number in case she had any more questions. Without hesitation, he gave her his cell number.

Even though Jeff didn't seem rattled, he was. He was desperate.

He had to boot Benny out of his house for good, before he could make even more trouble. Trying to evict Benny and Sonia in landlord-tenant court hadn't worked. Benny could still pay him to stay another twenty-one days, and Jeff couldn't wait any longer.

Jeff was going to try another tactic. Two weeks after the landlord-tenant court hearing, on a cold Friday afternoon, Jeff showed up at the rental house. Sonia opened the white aluminum screen door with an emblem of a black horse-drawn carriage on the front. Jeff handed her a letter: "I'm giving you $1,000.00 cash to vacate the property. . . . By accepting the $1,000.00 cash, you agree to vacate . . . by no later than January 31, 2009."

Sonia signed the letter and took the money.

5

BENNY HAD COME TO THE *DAILY NEWS* AND CONTINUED TO TALK TO US BE-CAUSE HE WANTED SOMETHING—TWO THINGS, REALLY. IN EXCHANGE FOR HIS story, he insisted on being anonymous. And he wanted us to put him up in a hotel or pay for housing, like some kind of witness protection program.

Barbara and I said no to both. Benny didn't get it—he was a convicted drug dealer with questionable credibility. And Benny wanted to be anonymous? This was a time of increasing public mistrust of the news media. Journalists had come under attack for using anonymous sources too liberally, à la Judith Miller, the *New York Times* reporter who was criticized for her stories about whether Iraq had weapons of mass destruction based largely on unnamed "American officials" and "American intelligence experts."

Of course we weren't the *New York Times*,

the great gray lady. We were the bawdy broad, a tabloid that lived—or died—off street sales. We never apologized for showing a little leg, in the form of a salacious sex story or a rubberneck tragedy—"grief porn," as some reporters called it—on our front page.

Still, we had our standards. There was no way we would agree to allow Benny, a convicted drug dealer, to accuse a decorated cop of wrongdoing without using his name. Benny had to go on the record.

When we told Benny this, he balked and left the newsroom. A few days later, he was back. "You're all I got," he told us.

Benny had gone to the Philadelphia Police Department's Internal Affairs Division, but he didn't think investigators took him seriously, nor did he trust them. He also shopped his story to Fox 29, but he didn't even get past the television station's front lobby.

We explained to Benny that the *Daily News* doesn't have a witness protection program, and certainly doesn't pay people for stories. We thought the FBI might be interested in Benny's story. We also knew that once the FBI started digging around, they wouldn't want Benny talking to us. So we milked Benny dry, talking to him for hours, with a tape recorder running.

When we were done, we steered Benny to the feds. We gave him the name and telephone number of John Roberts, the supervisory special agent of the FBI's Public Corruption Squad.

Roberts had a record of tackling police corruption. He was one of the FBI agents who investigated the Thirty-Ninth District police corruption scandal in the mid-1990s. In that probe, the feds charged five rogue narcotics cops with stealing money from drug suspects and covering up the thefts with phony arrests and search warrants.

History had a way of repeating itself in Philadelphia. And

Barbara and I suspected that what Benny was telling us could prove that those who fail to learn from history are doomed to repeat it.

To tell Benny's story, Barbara and I needed access to police search warrants.

Each search warrant would be a road map: it would list the address of the drug dealer, the dealer's name or street name, the amount and type of drugs purchased by the informant and how the deal went down, the badge number of every officer who participated in the raid, and what, if anything, police found in the house.

The warrants would show us what Jeff said he and other officers had witnessed to persuade a judge to authorize a raid. The paperwork would tell us whether Jeff used Benny as an informant, and what Jeff said Benny had bought in each house. These warrants would give us Jeff's version of events. Then we could ask Benny for his version of what happened. Finally, we could track down the arrested drug dealer or his relatives for their story.

But Barbara and I hit a roadblock. The city lawyer in charge of records requests was stonewalling us. We needed some legal muscle. The *Daily News* and *Philadelphia Inquirer* had just one full-time lawyer on staff. Scott Baker was an ambitious thirty-nine-year-old corporate lawyer when he joined our company as general counsel. Brian Tierney, the charismatic and peacockish CEO of the *Daily News*, the *Philadelphia Inquirer*, and Philly.com, wanted to grow readership and expand the business through acquisitions. Baker saw the job as a good opportunity.

But no one, including Tierney, could predict the crippling recession that put the newspaper industry on its knees. Lehman Brothers collapsed, and the economy tanked. The newspapers lost millions in advertising sales, and Tierney struggled to pay off the creditors who had lent him $350 million to buy the newspapers back in 2006.

Baker became mired in an effort to reach a deal with the lenders. Barbara and I would see him zipping through our newsroom, his eyes locked on his BlackBerry. He'd rush by and nod hello—a tall and trim blur in an Italian suit with salt-and-pepper hair. We e-mailed him: How can we get those search warrants? We called and left messages with his assistant: It's about the search warrants. Then e-mailed again.

Baker was working on our problem—ours and twenty others. The foundation of the newspaper industry was caving in, and all Barbara and I could think about were those damn search warrants.

Obsessive and antsy, we looked up the law pertaining to warrants. We printed out a copy of Pennsylvania's Rules of Criminal Procedure, which clearly stated that warrants, after police executed the search, were available for public inspection. The search warrants were stored in a dusty room on the fourth floor of the city's criminal court.

On Christmas Eve, just two weeks before Barbara went to landlord-tenant court, we walked over to the Criminal Justice Center with a copy of the rule on search warrants. The court staff was in the holiday spirit, eating cookies, drinking nonalcoholic eggnog, and getting ready to go home early. We found Marc Gaillard, the court's second deputy, and showed him the paper.

"Yeah, I know. I just talked to the city solicitor's office," he said.

"Woo-hoo!" Barbara yelped.

"Yaaay!" I said.

We sprang forward like two jack-in-the-boxes and grabbed Gaillard in a hug. Surprised, he took a step back, then smiled at us, probably thinking, These crazy *Daily News* ladies.

After Christmas, Barbara and I spent hours, days, in that dingy room, which was crammed with cardboard boxes, stacked floor to ceiling on metal shelves. Inside the boxes were yellow search warrants, thin as onionskin, crinkled and stuffed haphazardly into brown accordion folders. Written on each box in black permanent marker was the year, dating back to the early 1990s.

"Holy shit," I said as I sat cross-legged in jeans and sneakers on the dirty, school-cafeteria-like tile floor and looked through a box marked "Search Warrants 2006." Barbara paged through the wisps of yellow paper, periodically wetting her index finger with the tip of her tongue, while seated on a black milk crate in an electric-blue skirt and knee-high leather boots. My back ached as I flipped through hundreds of warrants.

We pulled three years' worth of search warrants, every one with Jeff's name and Benny's informant number. We ended up with stack a foot high—at least. We knew it would have cost the newspaper hundreds of dollars to order copies of all the search warrants, so we did it the *Daily News* way. We lugged reams of white copy paper from our office to the courthouse and befriended court employees on every floor. We charmed our way to their Xerox machines, and like a two-person army of leaf-cutter ants, we skittered in and out of the room to make copies, one search warrant at a time.

I had learned the art of getting something for nothing from my parents. At restaurants, my mom always asked the waitress for a plate of lemon wedges so she could make lemonade using water and sugar packets. My parents required me, my sister, and my brother to go to synagogue twice a year—on Rosh Hashanah and Yom Kippur, two holidays in which Jews sought repentance and atonement for past wrongs—but my dad refused to pay for tickets to attend services, so we snuck in through the synagogue's basement. As a teen, I sat in the pew, arms crossed, wearing a petulant scowl and an ugly floral dress, and rolled my eyes at my dad as the rabbi urged the congregation to start off the Jewish New Year with honest intentions. Later, when my rabbi, Fred Neulander, hired two hit men to bludgeon his wife to death in their Cherry Hill, New Jersey, home, my dad finally relented: Okay, we're done with synagogue.

When Barbara and I finished copying search warrants free of charge, we divvied up the stack and hit the streets.

Barbara and I went door to door, following MapQuest directions from one dealer's house to the next. Many of the homes were in West Kensington, a largely Puerto Rican neighborhood stricken by poverty and drug sales. It contained Philadelphia's most dangerous streets where bloodshed was so common it wasn't considered news.

Benny had told us which jobs were bogus, meaning that Jeff wrote in the search warrant application that he watched Benny make a buy at a certain house, but Benny told us he hadn't. He'd bought the drugs elsewhere—or not at all. Those search warrants, Benny told us, were lies.

We hit those homes first. We wanted to ask the dealers if they recalled anything unusual or fishy about the police raid. We thought we'd be less intimidating and have a better chance of getting people to talk to us if we went alone. So we split up and canvassed dangerous Philly streets taken over by drug dealers.

Snarling pit bulls, baring teeth and spewing saliva, lunged

at us. Wild-eyed, well-meaning crack addicts offered advice: "Honey, hope you gotta gun on youse, or at least some Mace." Drug dealers, wearing their version of business casual—tan Timberland boots, low-slung baggy jeans, and crisp white oversize T-shirts—told us to watch our backs.

"You know, you're in a bad neighborhood," drug dealers would tell us, as if we were naive adventurers who had wandered off across a border in search of designer knockoffs and good, cheap ethnic food.

Barbara chatted up drug dealers the same way she did her mail carrier. "You know I own this block," one drug dealer warned Barbara as she walked up the sidewalk.

"Well, that means you got my back, right?" she replied with a smile. Taken aback, he shook his head in amusement and chuckled.

At four-foot-eleven and ninety pounds, I took full advantage of my kidlike stature, even though I was pushing forty. I came across all pixie, with my Little Lord Fauntleroy haircut, flashing a puckish smile, but that was my secret weapon, perfect for disarming anyone from the career criminal to the corrupt politician. When I was out on the street reporting a story, I felt all badass—a legend in my own mind.

I had once picked up a just-freed convicted murderer and secreted him away in my house so I'd have an exclusive. At the time, I worked for the *Bergen Record* as a statehouse reporter based in Trenton. Another reporter got a tip that Thomas Trantino, dubbed New Jersey's most notorious cop killer, was about to be paroled.

Trantino spent almost forty years in prison for the execution-style murder of two police officers. In the early hours of August 25, 1963, Trantino and a friend, Frank Falco, raged out of control at a North Jersey bar. Lodi Borough police sergeant Peter Voto and police trainee Gary Tedesco arrived to investigate complaints of rowdiness. Trantino beat Voto on the head with a gun, and then ordered him to strip. When Voto disrobed too slowly, Trantino pumped him full of bullets while shouting, "We are going for broke! We are burning all the way! We are going for broke." Falco fatally shot Tedesco. New York police officers later shot and killed Falco while he was resisting arrest, and Trantino was sentenced to die in the electric chair. The US Supreme Court overturned the death penalty in 1972, however, and Trantino escaped execution. The state parole board, succumbing to public outrage, denied his parole nine times, making Trantino the longest-serving prisoner in New Jersey history.

Trantino's release in 2002, on his sixty-fourth birthday, was a big story for the *Bergen Record*. The slain cops had been from our region, and their relatives and friends still lived in our coverage area. The story was very competitive. Every news outlet in and around Manhattan wanted an interview with Trantino, the face of evil. Every editor wanted him first.

My editors picked me for the task. I was the newspaper's teeth-baring Chihuahua, but that's not entirely why they picked me. Trantino was being freed from a halfway house in Camden—less than two miles from my house.

My plan was to get to the halfway house ahead of the media horde. I set the alarm for 2:00 a.m., stopped at a WaWa for a large coffee, then parked my Honda Civic alongside a vacant lot across the street from the halfway house. The two-story brick building, surrounded by a tall metal fence, looked like a small jail. I sat in darkness, my coffee quickly cooling in the February air, and checked to make sure the car doors were locked. Camden had been ranked—yet again—among the top ten most dangerous cities in America.

Pretty soon, I had to pee. Damn it. I unlocked the door, stepped out of the car, and looked around. My best bet was the abandoned lot. I tiptoed around the clumps of knee-high weeds and nearly slipped on an empty beer bottle. I yanked down my jeans and underwear and squatted, then sprinted back to the car.

The sky turned from dark to pale gray, and by 9:00 a.m., I started to think the tip was bad. I didn't see any other reporters or TV news vans. I felt frustrated. Tired. Hungry. Bored.

Then I heard a rap on the car window. I looked up. An old man stood there. He had neatly trimmed white hair, a slim build, and a wrinkled face, and wore a gray sweatshirt and brown corduroy pants. I rolled down the window.

"I hear you're looking for me. The security guard told me you've been out here all night," he said.

Holy shit. It was Trantino.

"Yes. Yes," I said. "Get in. Get in!"

I leaned over and unlocked the passenger-side door. Trantino sank into the passenger seat, using his sneakered foot to move aside a crusty cereal bowl, flecked with dried oatmeal. Yesterday's breakfast. He dropped his black shoulder bag on the floor and eyed the dusty dashboard. A tangle of green, red, and black electrical wires hung from the car's busted mechanical sunroof. The windows leaked during rainstorms, and the seats stank of mold. The check-engine light, which reminded me of an orange throat lozenge, was on, as always.

"Man, your car's a mess," Trantino said.

Oh yeah, and you're a convicted cop killer, I thought.

I didn't want to piss him off. I also didn't want other reporters to get a hold of him. Where could I take him? Instinctively, I drove to my house. I lived just outside Philadelphia in a working-class, mostly white New Jersey town, a slice of Wonder Bread, where local cops worked hard to keep Camden's criminal element out. My Craftsman-style bungalow, with its leaky A-frame roof and faded yellow aluminum siding, sat under the flight path to the Philadelphia International Airport.

The house was quiet when Trantino and I walked in. Karl was at work; we didn't yet have kids. Trantino took in the living room, eyeing the black leather couch, hardwood floors, and shelves of art books. He noticed one of Karl's paintings, an abstract with red, orange, and yellow slashes, a depiction of a violent thunderstorm. Trantino sat at the dining room table. I made him a cup of hot chocolate and gave him a Jell-O pudding snack.

I asked the question I wanted to know most: Why?

"I can't believe that I did it. And that's the truth. I can't believe that I would kill anybody," he said.

We were wrapping up the interview when Karl came home from his job as an art director at an ad agency. Trantino stood and shook his hand.

"Tommy Trantino," he said.

I could tell that the name didn't register. Karl had no clue.

"Nice artwork," Trantino said, gesturing toward Karl's painting with a sweep of his hand.

While in prison, Trantino pursued an interest in poetry and art, particularly Asian art—Karl's favorite.

Karl and Trantino launched into a conversation about Khmer art, Buddha statues, Ganesha wall hangings. It wasn't long before the two men had their heads buried in one of Karl's many art history books. Trantino bragged that an art gallery owner in Tokyo wanted to present a show of his artworks.

"You should stay for dinner," Karl said.

Oh, crap, I thought.

"That's nice. Thank you. But I need to get going," Trantino said.

By then, another reporter, who had joined us, offered to drive Trantino back to Camden. Trantino said he had a line on an apartment there. He borrowed an art book from Karl. We never saw him or the book again. When I told Karl who Trantino was, he was miffed but not furious. We'd been married for three years, and he was used to my shenanigans. A year after Trantino's home visit, I signed up to cover the war in Iraq without first consulting Karl. It didn't occur to me that he'd be mad.

"C'mon, you know I would never volunteer to go to Iraq if we had kids. That'd be selfish," I argued.

Karl gave me a look, shaking his head. He wasn't buying my bullshit. He knew me too well. A good story was my drug.

Barbara drank from the same Kool-Aid.

She thought nothing of plunking down her credit card to buy a powder blue bulletproof vest for a ride-along with cops on drug raids. "Don't worry, honey," she told her husband at the time. "You'll see $795 on the Visa, but it's for a bulletproof vest, and the paper will reimburse me." She didn't get why the color drained from his face. He told her she had a serious problem.

Not long after that, Barbara had worn the vest as she shadowed narcotics cops into a crack den. Two little kids—one in diapers—sat on a soiled carpet, watching cartoons and eating Cheerios for dinner. A Phillies Blunt box filled with crack vials sat within reach. There was a filthy mattress strewn with lighters and matches. Barbara opened the refrigerator to find only ketchup, mustard, margarine, and wilted celery. She stood in the doorway as cops cuffed the glassy-eyed twenty-two-year-old mom. Her children sat just a foot away, with blank stares, their legs tucked under their tiny bodies. As cops led the mom outside, she walked by her kids, silent, not even looking at them. Barbara cried when she left the house.

The next morning, Barbara called the Philadelphia Department of Human Services to see if a social worker could check on the children. An intake worker told Barbara that parents who smoked and sold crack don't fit the city's definition of abuse or neglect. Barbara was incensed. She told Ed Moran, a reporter she had partnered with for the story, that she was going to check on the kids. He told her not to go, but she wouldn't listen, so he reluctantly went along.

The children were playing outside when they arrived. Their mom, released from jail six hours ago, sat on a stoop a few houses away. She shot Barbara a steely stare. Barbara knelt down and asked the kids, "How are you guys?" A cluster of drug dealers walked toward Barbara. To them, she was a busybody meddling with their business.

"Time to go, Barbara," Ed said, heading to the car.

"I'm not ready," she said, shooing him away with one hand.

"It's time," he shouted.

The young dealers closed in on Barbara. A few reached into the pockets of their baggy jeans.

"Barbara, NOW!" Ed bellowed in his thick Boston accent. Only then did she hop in the car.

So when friends and relatives asked Barbara and me if we were scared to knock on the doors of drug dealers, we didn't understand the question.

6

IN THE SEVEN YEARS THAT BENNY HAD WORKED WITH JEFF, THEY BEGAN TO LOCK UP SECOND GENERATIONS OF DRUG DEALERS. IN PHILLY, THERE were cop families and drug families. Children of cops wanted to wear the badge; children of drug dealers got sucked into an underworld of fast money.

The first house that Barbara visited belonged to Jorge Garcia and his family, whose names have all been changed in this book. Benny had told us that he'd never bought heroin from Jorge, even though the search warrant said otherwise. Jorge lived in the Badlands, a four-square-mile drug bazaar centered in West Kensington, home to the city's top three drug corners.

Drug dealers hung on corners while lookouts, teens on four-wheelers, sped around the block, looking for cops in uniform or street clothes. They yelled various codes as a warning:

Bomba! Aqua! Gloria! Five O!

This was corporate America of the streets, home to a multimillion-dollar business that had a finely tuned organizational structure. Above the corner boys were the holders, or guys who stashed the dope, and the caseworkers who picked up cash and delivered it to the drug bosses. Blood was spilled over turf wars. Little else.

By 2007, murder in the Badlands almost single-handedly gave Philly its nickname: "Killadelphia." That year there were 391 murders, the highest rate per 100,000 residents among the nation's ten largest cities, according to crime statistics compiled annually by the FBI. Gunshot wounds were so common that trauma surgeons from Sweden traveled to Philadelphia to learn lifesaving techniques they'd rarely need in their country. On average, one person was killed in the city every day. Many of these murders happened here in the Badlands.

When kids walked to school, they saw dealers pushing their brands. At Cambria and Hope Streets, the dope was known as Louis Vuitton. At Cambria and Master, Bart Simpson. At Cambria and Palethorpe, Seven-Up.

At Howard and Cambria there were two brands, Nike and Lucifer. This was the corner that never slept, one of the hottest drug spots in the city—and the most dangerous.

Most children at the elementary school on Cambria Street knew at least a few people who had been killed. Some were relatives. Kids as young as seven spoke of gunfire and blood on the street as if it were part of life; for them, it was. Every morning, school custodians swept up used condoms, needles, vials, and trash from the concrete play yard before children arrived.

Weathered memorials with teddy bears, balloons, and candles were scattered all over the Badlands. Sidewalks became street cemeteries. And these urban graves became part of the drug trade. Some dealers hid their heroin packets under worn stuffed animals.

A number of homes in the area were vacant or boarded up and reeked of pee and dead rats. Inside, addicts shot up, sitting on grungy mattresses or sofas with no springs. In the middle of some blocks, one or two houses had collapsed or been torn down to become weed-filled lots that looked like broken, missing teeth in a row of red brick. None of the battered homes on Jorge Garcia's block was worth more than a $15,000 used Chevy.

Barbara walked past the corner drug dealers and knocked on the door of the two-story redbrick row house with splotches of peeling cream paint. Jorge was still locked up, but his mom, Dolores Jimenez, was home. Dolores was suspicious of Barbara, almost hostile, but she was also curious about what Barbara had to say.

Family portraits in wood frames hung from the living room wall. A cross with Jesus on the crucifix was on the dining room wall, near a glass-top table with four chairs. Dolores's collection of black leather horses was inside an old wood cabinet. A playpen for her grandkids sat on the smudged linoleum floor. Two candles burned in clear glass. Her son Ricky's dusty basketball, baseball, and football trophies were scattered around.

Dolores's skin was sallow, and she moved slowly, as if her body hurt. That's because it did. Dolores suffered from high blood pressure, diabetes, asthma, a severe anxiety disorder, insomnia, and a ripped bowel duct. "They tried to take my gallstones out, but they messed up and now I have a stent in my stomach." She lifted her black T-shirt to show Barbara a dark, foot-long scar under her belly.

Dolores packed about 225 pounds on her four-foot-eleven frame. Her long black hair cascaded down to her waist, but most days she tied it back tightly in a ponytail, accentuating her full lips and large brown eyes that looked tired of the struggle. She wore no makeup, never did, except for a hint of black eyeliner every once in a while. Her nails were acrylic, perfectly rounded and finished in a natural shine, no color. She chose sweats in the winter, shorts in the summer, T-shirts always.

Dolores looked nothing like the other drug dealers that Barbara and I had met. When Barbara arrived, Dolores had just been released from prison on her own drug case. Eight years earlier, Jeff had busted her with Benny's help. Dolores was Benny's childhood friend, then a chunky, good-hearted, scruffy girl who went to church. Only a year apart in age, they rode the same school bus, and their moms were close friends. Later, she would become one of his drug suppliers.

Dolores didn't consider herself a drug dealer. In her mind, she was a thirty-six-year-old grandmom who dealt $20 bags of cocaine from her deep-pocketed black apron to make ends meet.

At the time of her arrest, she lived in a neighborhood on the cusp, just fifteen blocks from the Badlands. Her seven-room home was subsidized by the Philadelphia Housing Authority, and she got a welfare check. So did her twenty-year-old daughter Sofia, her firstborn. Problem was, Dolores told Barbara, there were so many children to feed and clothe. Dolores had four children. Sofia had her first baby at fourteen, followed by three more, all about a year apart.

Dolores had watched the mom across the street in disgust; the woman often left her seven kids alone with no heat so she could go "party."

"If you don't feed those kids, they'll take them away," Dolores warned her. Sure enough, she lost her children.

That would never happen to me, Dolores told herself. "I
take care of my kids."

Dolores raked in about $1,000 or so a week, wads of twen-
ties that gave her a taste of middle-class life. She bought a
minivan. She had the house painted and fixed up because
PHA seldom made repairs.

"I bought the kids designer clothes," she told Barbara with
a proud smile. "Polo, Nautica, Nikes, Air Jordans."

At first Dolores was nervous about selling drugs. But then
she shrugged; what the hell. It was easy, really. Her customers called her cell phone, said they'd stop by. She greeted
them at the front door in her apron, the same one she wore
to cook beans and rice or pan-fried chicken for her kids.
She wiped her hands on the black cotton, then gave them
ziplock bags of coke and folded their twenties into her apron
pockets. Some buyers made small talk, but they never stayed
long.

Business was brisk. Paydays were golden, like happy hour
at five on a Friday. All kinds came—blacks, Puerto Ricans,
whites from the Pennsylvania or New Jersey suburbs. In a
snap, she switched from Spanish to English in dope speak.
"No offense," she told Barbara, "but even Italians came," as if
somehow they were considered the drug world's elite.

She had been selling cocaine about a year when Benny
knocked on her door in 2001, while Jeff watched. It was Benny's first job as an informant.

Dolores wasn't suspicious, since she'd sold to Benny before.
She pulled a $20 bag of cocaine from one pocket of her apron
and put the cash in another. "It was like she had a little cash
register," Benny said.

Benny felt a tinge of guilt, but nothing more. "Jeff was telling me, 'You're doing the right thing. You're cleaning up your hood.' I told Jeff I felt bad, but he said, 'They're sellin' in front of their kids. They're going to end up just like them.' "

Dolores didn't see it that way. "Yeah. We got in the game," Dolores told Barbara unapologetically. "You get in the game to survive. And that comes with it, getting booked."

She figured she wouldn't sell forever, just a year or so more to stay afloat.

Dolores's brother, Manuel, who lived with her, also helped with the drug business. Until Jeff busted them, neither had a criminal record. Dolores's biggest crime had been a parking ticket.

Manuel had worked for more than twenty years at Today's Man, where he was a supervisor of the shipping and receiving department, making sure slacks, jackets, and button-down shirts landed in the right place.

At home, Manuel's closet was a shipping and receiving center—for cocaine. Everything they needed, including a metal sifter, digital scale, cutting agent, staples, and bags, was stored in a black leather bag.

It was four days before Christmas 2001, around 6:30 at night, when Jeff and his squad knocked on Dolores's front door. She cracked the door open and saw men she immediately figured were cops behind the iron-gated, locked storm door. She slammed the front door shut, scurried upstairs and flushed packets of cocaine down the toilet. In seconds, cops pried the steel apart with a crowbar and burst in.

Dolores's three-year-old grandson started to scream, terrified by a cop wearing a thin, silky black ski mask over his face. All anyone could see were his eyes. Some undercover narcotics cops who made buys wore masks during raids to conceal their identity, but Dolores's grandson thought a monster was coming after him.

Dolores said she'd never forget the way Jeff looked at her, like she was scum, or worse, a murderer. "It's like his shit don't stink, like he's better than everyone," she said. "It was like I was a nobody."

In Dolores's living room, cops found 119 packets of cocaine at the base of a baby stroller. They were tucked inside a Christmas cookie tin with a picture of Santa Claus on the cover. There was more upstairs. All in all, cops found $10,000 worth of coke in Dolores's house.

Prosecutors called her house a drug "operation." To them, it was people like Dolores who sank neighborhoods, smothered them like kudzu, that noxious coiling weed that quickly spreads over trees and shrubs until they die.

Dolores and her brother were sentenced to three to six years in prison. Guilt ate at her. Not for selling drugs, but because she couldn't be with her kids. "They was all lost souls," she said. Her worst fear was realized; her three youngest were alone. Jorge was sixteen, Ricky, fourteen, and Elena, eleven. Dolores asked her mom to take care of them, but she doubted that would work. Her kids drifted. Jorge, the one she'd nicknamed Macho as a baby, got locked up for violating probation on a gun case. Jorge's urine came back dirty because he was getting high on weed. The system couldn't save kids like Jorge. When he was released, there was no one, and that, in part, sealed his fate.

Jorge roamed the Badlands, the place Dolores knew was trouble for her kids. But there was little other choice. After the raid, Dolores and the kids were evicted from the Philadelphia Housing Authority house. Ricky, ever resourceful, even at thirteen, made a few calls to find a place for which the landlord didn't require references or job history. He found a three-bedroom house in the Badlands. The rent was $500 a month.

Dolores was still behind bars when Jeff locked up Jorge. It was 2005, and Jeff was no longer a stickler for rules. Jeff was sure he'd find heroin in Jorge's house. He just needed to get in there, and Benny knew exactly where to score dope. Benny purchased heroin from a drug house not far from Jorge's place, and Jeff used that heroin as the basis for a search warrant.

When Jeff and his squad raided Jorge's house, they found three bundles of heroin on top of a china cabinet in the dining room. They were stamped GAME CRAZY. In the back of a black dresser drawer, in a rear second-floor bedroom, cops found six clear plastic baggies of cocaine. Just shy of his twentieth birthday, Jorge was sentenced to two to four years in prison.

People like Jorge and his family almost always expected cops to lie, to be dirty, like pigs. They understood corruption. What they didn't understand was snitching.

"I'd rather someone stab me and let me bleed out before I'd become a fuckin' snitch," said Jorge's brother, Ricky, hate blazing from his eyes.

"He's a rat. And a rat should get poison," Ricky said, his lip curled as he almost spat out the words.

Ricky lived with Dolores and on this day, as Barbara interviewed her, Ricky sat by his mother's side, listening intently, interjecting frequently, as if Barbara was taking Dolores's deposition and he was her legal advisor.

Benny knew that we were going to talk to Jorge and drug dealers like him. He knew we were going to print that he was an informant, an informant who helped lock up dealers based on lies. And after we heard the venom spewed at Benny, we were surprised no one had killed him yet. It was then that Barbara and I realized that if Benny ended up dead, we'd be to blame. By talking to the dealers whom Benny had set up, we were salting the wounds.

Barbara sat across from Ricky at his dining room table and wondered what, if anything, he'd do to Benny. Ricky was shirtless, with low-slung black pants. He had a goatee, combed his short hair forward, close to his scalp, and had a space between his two front teeth. His arms, chest, and back were adorned in tattoos. Stretched across the top of his back were the words ONLY GOD CAN JUDGE ME above an unfinished cross.

Ricky seemed more upset that Benny played a role in his mom's drug arrest than in Jorge's. At fourteen, Ricky went to Dolores's sentencing, prepared to beg the judge for leniency. "I would have told him she did what she had to do. I don't blame her. People may see it as she was introducing me to drugs, but she raised four kids on her own, and how you gonna pay for all that? DPA don't pay for that."

Ricky was fiercely protective of Dolores, and he took care of her. Late at night or early in the morning, he slipped into her room, careful not to wake her, and placed food, usually a fruit yogurt, by her bed.

Dolores's life was unlike lots of others in the Badlands. She was born in Puerto Rico in 1965 and lived in a wood house with her parents and seven brothers. She was the only girl— "Daddy's little girl." Life was hard for her dad, who delivered Coca-Cola by truck. The family moved to Paterson, New Jersey, when she was four or five. "We came for a better life."

As a girl, she bounced around with her family, mostly

back and forth from Camden and Philly. Dolores hooked up with a high school boy, got pregnant with Sofia at sixteen, and dropped out. She met another man, Diego, when she was studying to become a nursing assistant. They had three children together, but had a turbulent, violent relationship. In the beginning he worked at a body shop, but he lost his job because he smoked crack all the time. He never worked again.

"I wanted to go back to being a nurse, but he didn't want that, so I didn't," Dolores told Barbara.

When he got mad or hallucinated, he hit or punched her, threw lamps at her. Even as a young kid, Ricky was her protector.

"I got in the way once. He cracked my head open. Here, feel this," he told Barbara, as he bent down and put her finger on his thick black hair. He wanted her to feel the bumpy scar tissue on the back of his head.

Dolores mustered enough courage to leave Diego when her dad got sick. "Poppy" was a diabetic with high blood pressure who endured heart surgery and suffered from Alzheimer's. She slept on a cot beside him in the hospital. When he couldn't walk, she stayed with him in rehab. She was the only one who shaved his face to his satisfaction. "He said his face had to feel like a baby's bottom." When he came home, she cooked him anything he wanted—hot dogs, boiled eggs, oatmeal, rice, and chicken.

He died on May 3, 1998, a Sunday. He opened his eyes, smiled at Dolores, then took his last breath.

Barbara understood Dolores more than she knew. Barbara's mom died of pancreatic cancer in November 2000. After she was diagnosed, Barbara did everything to save her. She begged a Mount Sinai Hospital researcher to include her in his coffee enema experiment. She knew it sounded ridiculous, but she was desperate. Her mom was seventy-three. She wasn't a candidate for surgery, and she refused chemo, said it would make her sicker. Barbara knew it wouldn't help anyway.

She wanted to die at home, even though she couldn't say the word *die*. "I want to go home," she told Barbara. And Barbara knew. She took a leave of absence from the *Daily News* and flew back and forth to Florida every week to sit beside her in bed all day and help her dad. Then she came home to take care of her two children because her husband needed to travel for work.

Barbara cooked her mom's favorite meal of roast chicken, boiled potatoes, and green peas. She spoon-fed her in bed while they watched her favorite reruns of *Law & Order*. When she could no longer chew, Barbara gave her broth, milkshakes, and Ensure. She sponge-bathed her, washed and brushed her thinning hair, and put lip gloss on her lips. As she slipped away, weighing not more than seventy-five pounds, Barbara stroked her cheek to trick her into opening her mouth so Barbara could slip in the painkiller Oxycontin. Barbara gave her more when she moaned. She changed her diapers. When her mom lost consciousness, she gave her Oxycontin in a dropper. Water in a dropper. Anything to keep her alive. Until the day Barbara knelt on the floor, held her limp hand, and told her it was okay to go. She'd take care of her brother and dad. Barbara didn't know if she heard her.

"How can my heart still be beating when hers isn't?" Barbara cried when her mom died two days later.

Soon after Dolores's dad died, she started selling drugs. When her mom died, Barbara fell into a deep depression that she tried desperately and unsuccessfully to hide. It was the beginning of the end of her marriage.

Death wasn't all Barbara shared with Dolores. Barbara's mom's mom was a four-foot-eleven Orthodox Jewish bootlegger who stashed cash under her mattress in her tenement at C and Eighth Streets on Manhattan's Lower East Side. Barbara's mom hid under the bed each time cops busted into their apartment and hauled her grandmother off to jail.

Her grandmom had a mission—her three sons and daughter would claw their way out of poverty and land careers to make her proud. When New York University had already filled their quota of Jewish medical students, her grandmom stormed down to the university with wads of cash in her purse.

"What does it take to get my son in?" she asked someone in the admissions office, in her Yiddish accent, plopping twenties on the counter. Barbara's uncle was accepted into med school and became a pediatrician. Another uncle became a rabbi; the other, an engineer.

Dolores and Ricky knew they came from a different world than Barbara. Ricky seemed curious about her home, her neighborhood. "When am I going to come see your land?" he asked her.

He told Barbara she must be comfortable. He thought Barbara lived in a mansion. She told him she lived in a three-bedroom home, nothing fancy.

"Don't bullshit me. Your three-bedroom home is different than my three-bedroom home," he said.

Ricky was right. She lived in a leafy, affluent Philly suburb just west of the city. The heart of her town was lined with trendy restaurants, with names like Plate and Verdad, and boutique shops that sold swimsuits year-round to rich housewives who went on winter cruises to tropical islands. Barbara's house, a three-bedroom brick colonial with blue shutters, sat on an ivy-manicured hill.

Unlike more than 90 percent of kids in Barbara's neighborhood, Ricky didn't have a high school diploma. "I didn't graduate, but I got brains like I did."

Ricky, who described himself as a "hard-core Christian," was cryptic about how he earned money, saying that he sometimes worked "off the books." He asked Barbara if she knew of any jobs.

Every so often, the conversation was interrupted by a knock on the door. Ricky would get up and furtively step outside for a minute or so. Dolores froze and lifted an eyebrow cautiously each time someone pounded on the door. The only person whom Ricky introduced to Barbara was "the Movie Man," an obese guy in a white T-shirt and jeans with a kind smile. Ricky sifted through his stack of pirated movies and chose some for himself and his mom—the street version of Netflix.

After the Movie Man left, Ricky brought the DVDs to Dolores and sat down at the dining room table. Barbara noticed he was staring at her hands.

"No ring?" he asked. "You're not married?"

"No. I'm not married."

"No?" he asked with a coy smile. "How could that be?"

"I'm divorced." Barbara still cringed when she said that word.

He asked about her children. She told him that her son, Josh, was in law school and her daughter, Anna, had just graduated from college and was working.

He stared at her, locking into her eyes. "You're still suffering from your divorce," he said.

The words took her aback. She didn't tell Ricky, but she still kept photos of her ex-husband in her wallet—one family portrait and one by himself.

"You need to get out more and live your life," he told Barbara. "You have your whole life ahead of you."

He paused. "You know what? We should go on a cruise."

"What?" she asked.

"You and me. A cruise."

In the span of an hour, Ricky asked Barbara to touch the back of his head, acted as her fortune-teller, gave her relationship advice, and asked her to sail away with him on the Love Boat. This was a typical day of street reporting for Barbara. On the other hand, when I went out on a story, people asked me if I came from a family of midgets or told me that I reminded them of Steve Urkel, the bespectacled nerdy character from the TV sitcom *Family Matters*. I'd think, Huh? But I'm white!

7

OF ALL THE PEOPLE BENNY BETRAYED, HE FELT THE WORST ABOUT HECTOR SOTO. HECTOR WAS LIKE A FATHER TO BENNY, MORE SO THAN HIS OWN DAD.

Benny's dad, Ventura Martinez-Perez Sr., was a local celebrity. He made Philadelphia history in 1971 when he became the first Latino officer on the city's public housing police force. He earned his FCC license at Temple University in 1976 and moonlighted as a Spanish-language radio announcer. On the airwaves, he talked sports, music, and politics. His on-air name was El Coqui, a type of frog in Puerto Rico that makes a racket.

Benny craved his father's affection and approval but knew he was a disappointment, even an embarrassment.

"My father always told me that I was a loser," Benny said.

Benny said his father once chased him down the street after he spotted him selling drugs on the corner. He kicked Benny out of the house and tossed all Benny's designer clothes—the Sergio Valente and Jordache jeans, leather blazer, Adidas sneakers—because he knew that Benny had bought the high-end threads with drug money.

Benny went to middle school with Hector's son, Noel, and Benny spent a lot of time over at their house. Hector and his wife, Lucy, were fond of the boy they knew as Flash. Benny and Hector shared a love of salsa music. Hector was a record producer who worked with some of the biggest names in Latino music; Benny took up the timbales and got regular gigs as a DJ.

When Hector wasn't recording music, he dabbled in drug dealing. He drove nice cars, wore neatly pressed slacks and Panama-style hats, and raised tropical birds. He was everything Benny wanted to be, and Hector took him everywhere in his 1976 Cadillac Seville, a two-toned light and dark blue beauty. They cruised through the neighborhood, driving past row houses with aluminum awnings draped with Puerto Rican flags. Brassy salsa music bubbled from front stoops, where old men sat talking or playing dominoes, flyswatter in hand, on folding chairs on the sidewalk.

Benny brought his girlfriends around to meet Hector, whom he introduced as "my pop." When Benny needed money to take a girl to a hotel, Benny called Hector, sometimes waking him in the middle of the night. Hector often gave Benny money for a hotel room, a movie, whatever. Hector's own son grew jealous. Noel couldn't understand why Hector never gave him money. The reason, Hector told Noel, was that Benny pestered him and whined until Hector opened his wallet.

Benny always spent Christmas Eve with Hector and his

family. Lucy made her famous Puerto Rican soup, a stew of black beans and garlic, and her shrimp *pastelillos*. Benny got drunk and spent the night on Hector and Lucy's couch. Lucy adored Benny. She would have let him move in, if he had asked.

In 1990, around the time that Benny was hustling $10 bags of coke on the corner, the cops nabbed Hector for selling cocaine out of his house. They confiscated twenty-nine grams of coke, a grinder, pestle, heat sealer, and scale. Hector landed in jail on felony drug charges. He posted $50,000 bail. While awaiting trial, he jumped bail and became a fugitive. At forty-three, Hector went on about his life, lying low but not hiding. He probably would have avoided prosecution and remained free—if not for Benny and Jeff.

When Benny turned police informant after Jeff busted him for selling marijuana and threatened to lock him up if he didn't, he didn't just flip—he transformed. He grew to like the power and got a rush from knocking on doors and conning his way into drug houses. He emerged from houses, drugs in hand, and strutted over to Jeff, bragging, "Man, I got these guys. They were supposed to be untouchable." Benny began to see himself as a cop, and Jeff grew to rely on Benny and treated him like a brother, or so Benny thought.

Over time, Benny's loyalty and alliance shifted from family friends like Hector to Jeff. Nobody killed Benny, because they hadn't figured out yet that he was a snitch. Benny was smoother than smooth.

In 2006—almost fifteen years after Hector became a fugitive—Jeff got a tip that he was selling drugs out of his corner row house. The house was a fortress. The front porch was caged by black iron bars. A surveillance camera, rigged to a television in Hector and Lucy's second-floor bedroom, was pointed at the front gate. Hector and Lucy described the camera system as a safety precaution in a dicey neighborhood, but Jeff knew that drug dealers used video cameras for countersurveillance on the cops.

It was 6:20 a.m., still dark out, on a chilly October morning. Hector and Lucy were asleep in their upstairs bedroom. The air-conditioning unit, cranked on high to alleviate Lucy's hot flashes, hummed and gurgled in the window. Lucy stirred slightly. Her barely conscious brain registered a muffled noise outside. *Thud. Thud. Thud.* Maybe the neighbor, hammering something. She had no idea that Jeff and seven other cops were at the front gate. Again and again, they slammed a battering ram into the metal lock until the wrought-iron gate banged open.

The cops came in like a freight train, roaring up the narrow staircase, single file, guns drawn. As they reached the second floor, Lucy opened the bedroom door. She stood, terrified, in her nightgown, barefoot.

A cop yelled, "Come down right now!"

She hustled down the steps to the living room. The cops burst into the bedroom and handcuffed Hector.

A cop shoved Hector to the ground. Hector fell on knees creaky and swollen with arthritis; he was an old fifty-nine. The cop struck Hector on the side of the head with the butt of a rifle. Hector's right ear, which later turned black and purple, took the brunt of the rifle. His ear throbbed.

From downstairs, Lucy heard Hector howl. She began to cry.

"Bingo!" one cop blurted. They found a clear, knotted sandwich bag, secreted in a dresser drawer, with fifteen ziplock packets amounting to 37 grams of cocaine, worth about $3,700 on the street.

A few days later, Lucy sat crying on the porch. With Hector locked up, she felt lost and scared. As she wiped tears from her cheeks, Benny happened by.

"Ma? Ma? What's the matter?"

"You didn't hear? They took Hector away, the cops, they took him."

Benny acted stunned. "If you need anything from me, if you need anything . . ."

Hector pleaded guilty to two felony drug charges: possession with intent to distribute and conspiracy. With the 1990 case still open, Hector could have gone to prison for twenty years. In exchange for his guilty plea, the judge sentenced him to three to eight years. They shipped him to a prison two hours away from Philadelphia.

Hector had been in prison for almost a year when Benny first came to the *Daily News*. Benny began to sob when he told Barbara and me about Hector. We believed he felt bad, but we struggled to understand how Benny could help set up someone so close to him.

On a cold January day in 2009, while Barbara tracked down Jorge's family, I drove from the *Daily News* to Hector and Lucy's house on the corner of Seventh and Lycoming Street. I knew from court records that Hector was in prison, but hoped Lucy was home. A gangly teen straddling a bike on the corner watched as I struggled to parallel-park my shrimpy car in a spot big enough to fit two Hummers. I got it on my second try, not too bad on the embarrassment scale, though the back bumper of my car stuck out, all hokeypokey, more than a foot from the curb.

Standing on the icy sidewalk, I was stumped by the iron bars encasing Hector and Lucy's porch. The gate was locked, and there wasn't a way to reach the front door.

"She not home," the teen called out. "You lookin' for Miss Lucy, right? She not home."

"Oh. Okay." I pulled out my reporter's notebook and scribbled a note, asking her to call me. I folded the note around one of my business cards and stuffed it in the gate lock. A few hours later, Lucy called and arranged for me to come over the next morning.

She greeted me at the gate. Lucy was a petite woman with bleached blond hair tied up in a ponytail. A girlish fifty-three years old, her face was smooth, except for a few faint lines that crinkled around her brown eyes when she smiled. A single freckle sat just above her upper lip.

Her living room looked like a white-and-black checkerboard. The popcorn ceiling and the plaster walls were painted a crisp white. The couch and chairs were a velvety black. The thick carpet was a sea of black. Everything else—the china cabinet, coffee table, end tables, knickknacks—was glass. We sat down at her dining room table. I gingerly placed my tape recorder and notepad on the pearl-colored glass table.

Lucy was eager to talk about Hector. She showed me a handmade Christmas card that he'd sent her from prison. On one side, he drew a heart and a rose with the words JUST LOVE underneath. On the other, he inked a portrait of them together, both smiling, with Hector's arm around her waist.

"I love him so much. You'd never believe how much I love that man," she said.

I told her what I knew. That Benny and Jeff set up Hector. Benny said he didn't want to buy from Hector, so he bought a $20 bag of coke from a guy who sold out of a nearby bar.

"For real?"

She thought about it for a minute, quiet. She narrowed, then widened her eyes, her face a fan of expressions that

changed from puzzlement to dismay. Lucy's reaction reminded me of the plastic volcano that my son Brody got for
Christmas. We spooned baking soda into the shot-glass-size
base, screwed on the tepee-like cone, and poured vinegar
into the narrow opening at the top. We watched as the white
liquid fizzed from the volcano's mouth and then bubbled
over in an angry cascade. I don't think the depth of Benny's
deception sank in until long after I left Lucy's house.

Later that evening, Hector called Lucy from the prison.

"Poppy, you know who did this?"

"Who?" Hector said.

"Flash."

"Flash. Flash? No. No, I don't believe it. He's like my son,"
Hector said.

Hector and Lucy would later throw out all the photos of
them with Benny. A photograph of Benny hugging Lucy went
straight in the trash. Lucy told me that Benny was raised in a
family with no love.

"We gave him love, and look what he did. . . . If you see
him, tell him that we don't want to see his face."

8

AFTER BARBARA ASKED JEFF ABOUT RENTING A HOUSE TO BENNY, JEFF HIRED A PIT BULL OF A LAWYER TO FEND OFF BARBARA AND ME. HIS SOLE job was to kill the story. Our job was to hold our ground.

On January 31, 2009, George Bochetto launched the first salvo in the form of a letter. The subject line read: "Urgent Warnings Regarding News Story." Just to make sure we got it, he sent the letter by fax, e-mail, and first-class mail.

"Officer Jeff _____ is an undercover narcotics officer with the Philadelphia Police Department, and is married and has two school-aged children living in Philadelphia. Any publication of Officer Jeff _____'s name, address, photograph, or any other facts which could lead to his identification or home address will place Officer Jeff _____, his wife, and his children in extreme danger."

We thought this argument was ludicrous. Jeff routinely testified in open court. He took the witness box and not only said his last name, but spelled it. When the prosecutor asked Jeff if he recognized the person whom he arrested, Jeff pointed to the drug dealer seated at the defendant's table. Jeff often made this identification in front of a courtroom full of other criminal defendants awaiting their own cases.

Bochetto also wrote that Benny's rap sheet read like a "credibility horror story," and he urged us to meet with him immediately.

On a late February afternoon, as heavy wet snowflakes fell, leaving faint pinwheels that quickly melted on the slick streets, Barbara and I stepped out of a cab in front of Bochetto's downtown law office on Locust Street. With boutiquish French glass doors, hunter green awning, and white stone entranceway, it was nestled among trendy restaurants, shops, and theaters.

I dressed for war. I ditched my size three and a half sneakers for tan leather pumps that I'd had to special-order from a shoe company called Cinderella. I swapped my owlish eyeglasses for contact lenses, put on crimson lipstick, eye makeup, and blush. I wore a plaid wool skirt and a purple V-neck sweater, with a brown scarf looped around my neck. Barbara, who had a wardrobe with clothes dating back to the 1980s, sported a black pencil skirt that she'd recently hemmed just above the knee, bringing the style into this decade. She paired it with a fitted jacket and her signature black leather boots, with the broken zipper and glued-on left heel. The Jewish hillbillies from Philly had arrived.

Once inside the reception area, we took a seat on a chocolate brown leather couch, tufted with buttons, the kind we imagined could be found in an English riding club. The decor was brut masculine, heavy on soft leather and dark wood. We waited for what seemed like a good while, at least one *Sponge-Bob* episode, I figured, using my kids' measurement of time. We wondered if the wait was intentional, if Bochetto wanted to make us sweat.

A skinny guy, with pasty skin and slicked-back black hair, approached us. He looked like a boy who had dressed up in his dad's pin-striped suit, which he paired, thoughtfully, with a blood-red silk power tie. A cross between Pee-wee Herman, a child vampire, and a pimp wannabe. He led us up a flight of steep, narrow stairs and ushered us into Bochetto's office.

Bochetto stood up from his massive, polished wood desk and shook each of our hands with a confident grip. He wore a smirk, an expression of amusement and curiosity. Clearly, he intended to make quick work of us. Bochetto's minion sat off to the side in a corner, with a yellow legal pad and pen on his lap.

We sat down across from Bochetto in matching teal-green upholstered chairs with deep seats and wood trim. When I sat back, the chair swallowed me up, clamlike, and my feet didn't touch the floor. I felt like Lily Tomlin as her five-year-old Edith Ann persona in a giant rocking chair. So I scooted forward and perched myself on the edge.

"Do you mind if I use my tape recorder?" I asked, as I placed it on his desk.

"No. No. You can't," Bochetto huffed. "That's a violation of Pennsylvania's Wiretapping and Electronic Surveillance Control Act."

I started to protest, but he cut me off. "This conversation is off the record."

"No," I said, petulant and defiant.

He looked at me incredulously. We could see him begin to simmer.

"I'm sorry, but we can't agree to that," Barbara said.

Ding. Ding. We were in Bochetto's boxing ring, and round one had begun. The fiery attorney liked to fight. He was a fighter from the moment he was born.

As an infant, Bochetto was abandoned at a Brooklyn orphanage and spent the first seven years of his life without a last name. He cycled in and out of foster homes and fell prey to street punks who teased him and beat him up. A family from Rochester, New York—the Bochettos—adopted him. The scrawny teen found a second home in a nearby gym, where he taught himself to box, punching a weight bag to toughen himself up—inside and out. Bochetto became an amateur boxer and later graduated, cum laude, from Temple University School of Law in 1978. Then-governor Tom Ridge appointed Bochetto state boxing commissioner in 1995, and the Pennsylvania Veteran Boxers Association named him Man of the Year in 1997. As boxing commish, Bochetto raised money to open gyms and boxing leagues in neighborhoods battered by violence. He dug into his own pocket to pay gym fees for poor kids.

The fifty-six-year-old Bochetto oozed panache and power. Under other circumstances, we might have thought him handsome, in his stylish dark-framed eyeglasses and starched white dress shirt embroidered GEORGE near the breast pocket. He combed his thick graying hair back in a wavelike ripple.

His office was a shrine to boxing. The dark green walls were decorated with posters of legends like Muhammad Ali and Mike Tyson and photos of Bochetto with them. Silk boxing trunks autographed by Ali and Joe Frazier hung on the wall near oil paintings of fighters. Boxing gloves were displayed in an antique china cabinet with a glass door. On Bochetto's desk sat a 1936 bronze sculpture of clashing boxers.

The work, entitled *The Uppercut,* was created by boxer-turned-artist Joe Brown. A black T-shirt sold during the 1995 fight between Mike Tyson and Buster Mathis Jr. was preserved in a picture frame. As boxing commissioner, Bochetto had licensed Tyson to fight in Pennsylvania after Iron Mike got out of prison for rape, paving the way for the Philadelphia Tyson-Mathis matchup. On a side table was an original, unopened Wheaties cereal box with Ali on the front.

Bochetto, who specialized in libel law, began to lecture us, his voice laced with anger and frustration. He couldn't understand why we would even consider writing a story based on the word of a convicted drug dealer turned informant.

"What do you guys think you are going to do? Win a Pulitzer Prize?" he sneered.

Of course drug dealers arrested by Jeff, a decorated cop, would say that Benny never made the buy. They'd feed us any bullshit to beat the case, and Benny was a bottom-feeder, Bochetto told us.

"Being a confidential informant, those are spaces occupied in the main by scumbags," Bochetto said. "These are liars and thieves and snakes who will do anything and say anything for any reason. They never man up. They never face reality and accept the consequences. They are always looking for a crack to crawl in, a rock to crawl under."

Any reasonable person, anyone playing with a full deck, would have got Bochetto's point and probably dropped the story.

Not us. Maybe we were off our gourd, but we knew that Jeff had rented a house to Benny. I mean, Barbara had been at landlord-tenant court. We believed that Jeff had lied on some of the search warrants. They read alike, as if they were cookie-cutter form letters that Jeff filled in with different names and addresses, a kind of Mad Libs. And we weren't the only ones who thought that the search warrants smelled. Veteran and smart attorneys like Stephen Patrizio, who had represented Raul Nieves and figured out Jeff had rented a house to Benny, thought so, too.

And no one—not even Bochetto, this hardscrabble bully with his commonsense argument—could convince us otherwise. This was why Bochetto was worried. He knew we were trouble. We lacked the skepticism and doubt that Bochetto had seen in other seasoned reporters. He sensed our enthusiasm, our energy. He could tell we were enjoying this fight, though he was convinced we'd lose.

He leaned forward, his arm extended over a Civil War–era sword—a gift from a client—that sat in the middle of his desk. He jabbed his index finger, first at me, then at Barbara. "I'm going to sue you—and you—personally!"

We stood up to leave. I whipped my scarf over my left shoulder and shook his hand. "It's been a pleasure," I said, rolling my eyes. My sarcasm elicited a little snort, almost a chuckle, from Bochetto.

We climbed into a cab and looked at each other, wide-eyed.

"Do you think he can sue us? Personally?" I said.

"Geez, I hope not. We'd lose our houses. Wendy, we'd be homeless," Barbara said.

We began to giggle nervously.

"Nahhhhh!" I said.

Barbara and I did cede some ground to Bochetto. He had chastised us for not contacting officers and supervisors who could vouch for Jeff's character. We realized he was right. Bochetto agreed to e-mail us names and numbers of Jeff's colleagues, and we agreed to send him a list of our questions for Jeff.

Bochetto sent over the list of people he described as "more than willing and anxious to provide you with direct, firsthand knowledge of important facts relating to your article." We hit the phones the minute we got the list. Richard Eberhart was the first name. Eberhart was Jeff's former partner. He had retired a few years earlier and now, along with Jeff, owned J&R Dunk Tank Rentals, a company that rented moon bounces and carnival games for kiddie parties.

Barbara called Eberhart on his cell. Not surprisingly, Eberhart described Jeff as "an excellent police officer, a straight shooter, a hard worker, an all-around good guy." She asked Eberhart if he thought Benny was credible and reliable. When Eberhart said, "Yes," Barbara began to feel the endorphins of a reporter's high, a blend of panic attack, sugar rush, too much caffeine, and great sex.

"Did you know that Jeff rented a house to Benny?" she asked, and threw in, as if a casual afterthought, "What did you think of that?"

"Would I have done that? Probably not. But who am I to judge?" Eberhart said. "I thought he was helping him out. It didn't seem inappropriate at the time, but looking back, maybe it was."

Barbara hung up and zoomed over to my desk, flapping her arms like a seal just before the zookeeper tosses a fish. "You're never gonna believe this," she said.

"Get the fuck out!"

We sent Bochetto our questions, fourteen in all, and to tweak him further, we gave him a deadline—highlighted in bold—of 5:00 p.m. the following day. He must have wanted to box our ears.

Bochetto didn't answer a single question, but he gave us a colorful and snarky quote: "It is overwhelmingly clear that, when the hard facts are put on the table, your story falls apart and your questions become empty vessels of naïveté. What you have, and what you apparently want to rely upon, are nothing but a self-serving series of fictionalizations by professional liars, felons, and drug addicts, each of whom are looking to avoid more jail time by playing the *Daily News* for a patsy."

Barbara and I labored over writing the story. We spent hours together in front of the computer, surrounded by documents, interview notes, and empty coffee cups. The floor underneath my desk was littered with Rice Krispies Treats wrappers. At ninety calories apiece, the marshmallow sponges were the only junk food that Barbara allowed herself to eat. I bit my fingernails and gnawed at the cuticles until they bled. I would have salted myself and chewed off my fingers—if I didn't need them to type.

The story was a sprawling tale about how Jeff and Benny met, their rental arrangement, and Benny's allegations that Jeff fabricated evidence to get into drug homes.

9

OUR IRASCIBLE CITY EDITOR, GAR JOSEPH, WAS HOLED UP IN HIS CLOSET-SIZE OFFICE FOR WHAT SEEMED LIKE HOURS. WE WEREN'T SURE IF THAT WAS a good thing or bad; we just knew that he was in there reading a draft of our story. Actually, it was draft number four.

Gar had declared our first version "a fucking mess." He wasn't the type of editor to tiptoe around reporters' fragile egos. He got impatient, sometimes unapologetically rude, with reporters who couldn't pitch a story idea in one sentence or less.

"I have no idea what the fuck you're talking about," he'd say. "Can you tell me again—in English."

As city editor, Gar was the first stop for rough drafts, and often the last. "This story ain't gonna run, unless you can figure out a way to make it unboring." The sixty-year-old former City Hall reporter with a salt-and-pepper goatee had been around so long that he didn't think anything was story-worthy. Here's an e-mail he sent to editors assigned to work on Thanksgiving: "I don't give a shit about the [Thanksgiving] parade unless a small child is entangled in the ropes of the Mighty Mouse balloon and choked to death, so don't waste a reporter on it."

Gar walked toward Barbara and me with his trademark limp, the result of running too many marathons.

"I think you've got something really good here," he said, waving us into his office. A sticker that read "Easy Sucks" was taped to the glass panel beside the door. We sat on his ratty, gamy-smelling couch as he called up the story on his computer. His idea of a motivational poster hung on the wall: "Despair. It's always darkest just before it goes pitch black."

"The story's way, way, waaaaaay too long. This section here veers off a cliff," Gar said.

Gar despised long stories. He believed the Bible could be boiled down to six words. "Old Testament: 'God is great.' New Testament: 'God is love.' Bam, done. Of course, you lose some of the metaphors," Gar liked to say.

He also hated stories written in esoteric geek-speak.

"This part doesn't make any fuckin' sense," Gar told us, as we stared at the blinking cursor on his computer screen. "It's written in mumbo-jumbo police jargon that no reader's gonna understand.

"Other than that, it's pretty good. Fixable," he sniffed.

After a two-hour-long journalistic colonoscopy on a cold, rainy Friday night, Gar leaned back in his swivel chair, adjusted his eyeglasses, folded his arms across his chest, and said, "Now let's see what our lawyer has to say."

We weren't sure the story would ever run, or when the lawyer would read it.

Thinking we had done all we could do before the weekend,

Barbara left work at about 6:30 p.m. to go on yet another blind date.

She'd been divorced for more than three years and was tired of being alone or stuck in relationships that she knew, deep down, weren't quite right. She signed up for Match.com and spent hours crafting her profile. She began, "I'm the kind of woman who likes to pack a lot into each day so I can go to bed at night with a smile on my face, knowing I truly live."

When she showed me her profile, I blurted, "Oh, Barbara, that's soooo schmaltzy. You gotta change that."

She looked crushed and later went home and rewrote the top. Not surprisingly, Barbara's profile generated dozens of electronic "winks." She quickly realized that winkers fell into two camps: shy, insecure types who were interested but wanted her to return the wink before they wrote a note; or fishermen daters who cast a huge net and winked at hundreds of women to see who bit.

Some nights after work, we'd sit at Barbara's desk and she'd pull up the latest dating prospects. We scanned their photos and bios. Some made us laugh, others made us cringe, and a few went in the "not bad" category. One with a username something like "sexyfunsmart77QX" looked neither sexy, fun, or smart. Another resembled a wild-eyed Charlie Manson who might stuff her body in a trunk. He wanted to meet for a drink. She visualized her blood in a glass. Two more were not much older than her twenty-two-year-old son, Josh. "We'd be great together, gorgeous," one wrote. We knew where he wanted to be "great." The last one had an anger-management problem: "The LEAST you could do is write back. Your loss!"

The guy she planned to meet on that Friday night sounded promising. He had told her that he was a fifty-four-year-old manager for a computer company, had two adult kids, and loved to run. She met him at a coffee shop.

This couldn't be him, she thought, as she saw this man, mostly bald, with a few strands of gray hair swept to the right in a comb-over, walk toward her. With tense, slightly hunched shoulders and a slow gait, he looked close to Barbara's dad's age. Nothing like his Match photo. He said in his profile that he was six feet tall. Maybe thirty years ago, Barbara thought.

He stretched out his liver-spotted hand for her to shake, and they walked inside.

Within twenty minutes, he pulled out his wallet to show Barbara photos of his three grandkids. They were next to his AARP card. He told her he had retired from his job.

"So how old are you?" she asked curiously.

"Sixty-six," he said.

"But your profile says you're fifty-four."

"I know. I figured most women your age would dismiss me if I put my real age. And all they have to do is meet me."

"But that's a big age difference. That's like twelve years," she said.

"You know what?" he said, leaning toward her, clearly irritated. "Most women your age have no problem with it. I have a five-bedroom house, a pool. I drive a Mercedes, have a boat. The last woman I dated was forty-eight."

Barbara looked at her watch.

At about 7:30 p.m., I was just shutting down my computer when Gar came over to my desk and said that our attorney, Scott Baker, and Michael Days, the paper's top editor, wanted to go over the story. Right now.

I thought about calling Barbara but didn't want to interrupt her date. Loaded down with an armful of documents, I trailed Gar, beetle-like, into Michael's glass-front office.

Michael waved me in and I took a seat at the conference table. Scott had inked up a copy of our rough draft; he'd circled words and phrases that he deemed too loaded and scribbled notes and question marks in the margins. We went over the story, line by line. I slid documents—search warrants, interview notes, Bochetto correspondence, the rental agreement, and the landlord-tenant eviction notice—across the table for Scott's review.

"Do you think we are going to get sued?" I asked.

"There's a fifty-fifty chance," said Scott, who pointed to Benny's criminal record. "The guy is a convicted drug dealer."

"Yes, I know," Michael said, "but these are two fine reporters. Ultimately, you have to trust your reporters." He turned to me. "What does your gut tell you? Do you believe him?"

"I do," I said.

"To me, it passes the smell test," Michael said about Benny's story.

Fear of a libel lawsuit, said Scott, is not a good enough reason to kill a story. "This is a newspaper. You're a reporter. We're in the business of writing stories."

I felt the urge to hug this corporate lawyer, this unexpected ally and champion of journalism.

Barbara and I came into the office on Sunday to fact-check the story one more time. Barbara called Bochetto to let him know that the story was slated to run the next day. She asked if he had any additional comment. He had none. Gar gave the story a final read. Kevin Bevan, the editor in charge of the page-one design, who wore a down-on-the-farm plaid flannel shirt to work every day, showed us the headline he coined: "Tainted Justice?" The question mark was a hedge, the *Daily News* version of a wink, as if just askin'—"Hey, readers, do you think this cop is corrupt?"

"You can commit a lot of sins with a question mark," Bevan once said, half joking. The *Daily News* was famous for slapping question marks on headlines. "Trish's Killer?" on a story naming a homicide suspect. "Armed & Angry?" on a story about cops arresting NBA star Allen Iverson on gun and assault charges. "A Veteran Kidnapper?" "Devil in Blue?" "Highway Robbery?" It fit when we believed a criminal, politician, or public figure was guilty in the court of public opinion, but not yet charged.

The front-page mock-up that Kevin showed us featured a grainy silhouette of Benny, with a hoodie pulled tight around his face. The photograph, filmed against the backdrop of the paper's dimly lit loading dock, had a sinister feel. The headline blared, "A Cop and an Informant Got Too Close and Bent the Rules. Now, the Informant Fears for His Life. Tainted Justice? Page 3."

We believed Jeff was a dirty cop. No question. And every story we wrote after that first one carried the moniker "Tainted Justice." Fact.

The next morning, we came to work prepared to take some heat for the story. We never expected the hair-singeing, ass-burning thermonuclear fireball that would soon unfold.

10

BARBARA AND I IMMEDIATELY LANDED
ON THE FBI'S MOST DESPISED LIST.

"Our investigation is in the toilet," a
miffed FBI agent told me the day our story
ran.

The feds were mad that we had convinced
Benny to tell his story and then pointed
him in their direction. "I realize that you
guys have a job to do," the agent conceded,
adding that he wished Benny had gone to
the FBI first and not the other way around.

In the days before our story ran, Benny
sat down with the feds and they wired him
up in hopes of snagging Jeff on tape. They
wanted Jeff to admit that he had phonied
up arrest paperwork and perjured himself
in court. Benny told Barbara that the feds
had given him a keychain, rigged with a
miniature tape recorder. When Jeff arrived
at landlord-tenant court, Benny confronted
him in the hallway and tried to goad him
into a confession. Jeff was leery; he gave

up nothing, and we didn't help matters. When Barbara approached Jeff after the eviction hearing, he knew Benny had sicced us on him. He wasn't stupid.

The Internal Affairs Division was equally rankled. Police commissioner Charles Ramsey railed that we'd blown their cover, forcing investigators to abandon their undercover operation. Ramsey had no choice but to strip Jeff of his gun and police powers and put him on desk duty. Ramsey transferred Jeff to the Roundhouse—the hatbox-shaped police headquarters building, where Jeff spent all day taking fender-bender accident reports over the phone. Without the opportunity to use a wiretap, the probe would take months as investigators painstakingly dissected every job Jeff did with Benny.

As vexed as internal affairs was by us, they were even more furious at Benny for going over their heads.

When Benny went to the feds before giving the police department time to investigate, he might as well have flipped all of internal affairs the bird. But that was Benny. He worked all the angles until he got what he wanted, or in his mind, what he needed. His alliances were on spin cycle.

When Jeff told him that he had to get out of his house, Benny went to internal affairs. When internal affairs didn't whisk him into witness protection, he went to Wellington Stubbs at the Philadelphia Police Advisory Commission. When Barbara and I told him that we couldn't write his story without using his name, he went to Fox 29. When the FBI asked him why he went to the *Daily News*, he rolled Wellington under the bus.

"I only did what Wellington told me to do," Benny shrugged, as if he had no clue that the FBI and internal affairs wouldn't be happy with Wellington. When the city's deputy mayor learned that Benny got my name from

Wellington, he scolded Wellington for exercising poor judgment. The city later forced Wellington to resign. Wellington believed the city fired him in retaliation for sending Benny my way, but the city claimed Wellington had violated a rule requiring city employees to live within Philadelphia.

Benny was good at playing victim. Once, after FBI or internal affairs investigators picked him up in a car without tinted windows, Benny bitched to us that they didn't give a shit about his safety.

"Jeff might have been an asshole with me and jammed me up, but he always picked me up in a tinted car. He was protecting me," Benny complained to me.

When the FBI wouldn't help him out with money or housing, Benny claimed they were punishing him for talking to us. The guilt ate at us because we cared about Benny and his family. His kids were close in age to mine, and I agonized that the story had put them at more risk. For me, telling Benny's story came at a price—I would forever feel responsible for his safety, despite all his faults. I often found myself caring about people I wrote about, but usually they were sympathetic characters. Benny was not.

It didn't bother me and Barbara when FBI and police heaped blame on us. They had their job; we had ours. Our job was to shine a white-hot light on wrongdoing.

In the early 1980s, there was the One Squad scandal—a small circle of narcotics officers were convicted of selling drugs they stole from dealers. Then, in the late 1980s, came the Five Squad Scandal—four officers in an elite narcotics squad went to prison on federal racketeering charges for taking bribes from drug dealers. In the 1990s, there was the Thirty-Ninth District scandal—a half dozen narcotics cops pleaded guilty to framing and beating suspects, lying under oath, and robbing drug dealers. The Thirty-Ninth District scandal was an iceberg that ripped open the hull of the criminal justice system and sank the public's trust in narcotics cops. Hundreds of cases got tossed or overturned, and the city paid millions of dollars to settle federal civil rights lawsuits filed by people wrongly arrested and jailed.

Cops who worked narcotics were especially susceptible to corruption. For one thing, narcotics cops faced a Sisyphean task, an endless and hopeless battle to stem a tsunami of drugs. The dealers literally outgunned and outnumbered the cops, so why play fair? Why not cut some constitutional corners to gain the upper hand? Day in and day out, narcotics cops arrested gun-toting dealers who raked in thousands of dollars a week, drove luxury cars, and adorned themselves with fur coats, jewelry, and designer clothes, while the cops were risking their lives and slogging out a living on a $50,000-a-year cop's salary. If they helped themselves to some drug money or pocketed a diamond ring or framed suspects to boost their overtime pay, what did it matter? Didn't they deserve additional compensation? Corrupt cops were unapologetic.

After each scandal, police watchdogs and civil rights lawyers cited poor training, failure to discipline, and lax rules and oversight of cops who worked with drug informants. They made recommendations for reform—and the police department largely ignored their suggestions. The fact was, Benny didn't trust internal affairs because its investigators had a history of failing to police their own.

If police brass and internal affairs wanted to blame Barbara and me for blowing their investigation, fine. But if they had cleaned their own house years back, we wouldn't be here. That's how we saw it.

The Defender Association of Philadelphia, which represents

poor people in criminal cases, began to scrutinize scores of drug cases in which Jeff used Benny as an informant. In the wake of our first page-one story, civil rights attorneys clamored for more supervision of and better training for narcotics officers. The police inspector in charge of narcotics lamented that the allegations, if true, could free dozens of drug dealers, casting a black cloud over the entire narcotics field unit. And the city district attorney's office launched an investigation into Benny's allegations. A few days later, the mayor, the FBI, police internal affairs, and the Philadelphia Office of the Inspector General announced the formation of a joint task force. During an afternoon news conference, city mayor Michael Nutter, whose nasal voice reminded me of Kermit the Frog, especially when he was trying to sound firm, said he wouldn't hesitate to come down hard on Jeff if the investigation revealed wrongdoing.

"We think that high ethical standards matter in the entire city, but especially in the Philadelphia Police Department," said Nutter, grim-faced. "If any of these allegations are true, we will take, I'm sure, the swiftest action."

"Obviously, ensuring the safety of individuals involved in this investigation will be paramount," Janice Fedarcyk, FBI special agent in charge, said at the press conference when reporters asked about witness protection for Benny.

By now, the age-old *Daily News–Inquirer* rivalry was in full tilt. *Inquirer* editor Bill Marimow had won not one but two Pulitzer Prizes—in 1978 and 1985—for an investigative series that exposed police brutality and misconduct. This was his kind of story, and he wanted his paper to own it. The *Inky* reporters weren't going to follow us, they were going to beat us. Within two weeks, the *Inky* had seven reporters on the story. The sleeping giant was wide awake.

When *Inky* deputy managing editor Vernon Loeb thought

that his reporters did a better job than us on their follow-up story about the fallout from Benny's allegations, he dashed off a congratulatory e-mail from his BlackBerry and copied all the top editors:

"While I never liked getting beat on a story (and I'm not saying it was you two guys who got beat on the original *Daily News* piece about [Jeff and Benny]), I knew it was an occupational hazard, and you could never break every story. But I always vowed to myself that I'd never get beaten on a follow, and I always loved to take over the stories I was beaten on and mercilessly pound my competitors once I was on the case. And this is why I absolutely loved—loved!—this scoop you guys had this morning, significantly advancing this important story and announcing to the *Daily News*, with data analysis they can't possibly match, that we're not going to be beaten again, and that we in fact intend to own this story from here on out. Great work. Best, Vernon."

The e-mail became a running joke in our newsroom. *Daily News* columnist Howard Gensler, who wrote the paper's celebrity gossip du jour, slipped the phrase "mercilessly pound" into a column about how *Extra* beat out *Access Hollywood* and *Entertainment* as the first to report that Nicollette Sheridan was leaving *Desperate Housewives*.

It was ridiculous that reporters at the two newspapers—owned by the same company, operating out of the same building—regarded one another as competition, even enemies. Ridiculous, that is, to everyone but us.

When the *Daily News* scooped the *Inquirer* on a story, *Inky* editors dressed down their reporters. "You got beat, don't let it happen again." When they scooped us, our editors minimized their victory. "Well, you know, they have more people, more resources."

The *Daily News* harbored an inferiority complex, fueled by the fact that some of our reporters had applied for jobs at the *Inquirer* and didn't get hired and that *Inky* staffers made more money. When I parachuted down to the *Daily News* to avoid being laid off in late 2006, I got to keep my $76,648 *Inquirer* salary, which meant I made more than some *Daily News* reporters who had been with the company longer. Barbara, who was my editor at the time, made only $4,316 more than me, even though she had worked at the company a decade longer. The *Daily News* was a second-class citizen, and that made our victories somehow sweeter. The Goliath *Inquirer* looked down at us from its perch as we bobbed and weaved, swinging hard. Occasionally, we got our jabs in.

Some *Inky* reporters viewed our mangy troupe as a pest, a persistent termite problem within their stately institution. They secretly wanted us to close, and whenever company number crunchers talked about folding the *Daily News*, the *Inky* reporters wished it so, though they'd never say the words aloud.

At the venerable and cultured 180-year-old *Inquirer*, I was like a kazoo in a symphony. "I'm your bitch," I once told a reserved editor who asked me to help cover the deadly shooting of five Amish children at their Lancaster schoolhouse. There was silence on the other end of the phone. He didn't know how to take my comment, which was just my quirky and profane way of telling him, "Look, I'll do whatever you need." Once, when Karl came down with epididymitis, a painful inflammation of the testicles, I told my editors that I had to leave early because "my husband's balls are killing him." They shook their heads as I shut down my computer.

The "mercilessly pound" e-mail egged us on, feeding our desire to kick some *Inky* ass.

Barbara's will to win, the force within her that drove her

to cross the finish line in three marathons, was the fuel that made her a tenacious reporter.

She wasn't a natural athlete. Far from it. As a teen, she was klutzy, always among the last to be picked for a volleyball or basketball team. When she had to do a routine on the uneven bars in a high school gym class, she got stuck on the top bar, her feet and head dangling hopelessly as the bar cut into her stomach.

By the time she reached her twenties, she got out of breath walking up stairs and felt out of shape. She decided to start running. The first day she couldn't make it three blocks. It took her a month to build up to a mile. She ran at such a slow pace, walkers passed her. She stuck with it and even ran during the first six months of being pregnant with her son, Josh.

To train for a marathon, she got up before dawn and, donning a reflector vest, headed outside, whatever the weather. Some days she ran the same hill eight times over. She seemed to get a sick pleasure out of pushing her body to its limit. She ran the New York City Marathon with an overtraining injury. At mile 20, her legs and feet had turned to lead. Every step felt like daggers piercing through her calves and thighs, but she knew she'd get to the finish line, even if she had to crawl. In every marathon, the last 6.2 miles are killers, the ones where the body checks out and the mind takes over.

Barbara fed off the human chain of 2 million spectators who lined the 26.2-mile course—men, women, and children, three layers thick, who let out a deafening, thunderous roar for Barbara and other average joe runners as if they were Kenyans. They held out their hands for runners to high-five. Barbara slapped hand after hand, using that human connection to tell herself she would not, could not quit.

In the last mile, tears came to her eyes. She saw flashes of her life, but only the good parts, like the moments her children were born and she held them for the first time. All she heard was applause. "Keep going. I can't do what you're doing," yelled one man who caught her eye.

Then she saw the packed bleachers, the blue banner, and the time clock. The finish line.

Barbara would go for a run on frigid mornings, the cold air burning her nose and eyes. She flexed her stiff fingers, wrapped in gloves emblazoned with the words I KNOW I RUN LIKE A GIRL. TRY TO KEEP UP.

Barbara approached her job like a marathoner. Stuck to her computer, she kept a Winston Churchill quote: "Never Never Never Give Up."

We were the underdogs. The B team. The long shot. We weren't expected to win. The thing was, Barbara and I both hated to lose.

11

LESS THAN TWO WEEKS AFTER OUR
FIRST STORY RAN, BARBARA AND I
CAME INTO WORK TO FIND AN AVA-
LANCHE OF HATE E-MAILS.

"You fucking piece of shit!" one reader
wrote. "You are a disgrace to yourself and
your family and this city!" The reader continued, "It's a shame that you have an ability to get the word out about the positives of
this police department . . . and this is how
you earn your money."

We understood the root of their anger.
A North Philadelphia drug dealer, Thomas
Cooper, aka Thomas Smith, was poised to
walk free because Jeff and Benny were tied
to his case.

Jeff and Benny often targeted nickel-
and-dime drug peddlers. This case was different. Thomas Cooper—twice convicted
on felony drug charges—was big-time.
When Jeff and his squad raided his house,
they found a stash of drugs, including 155.6

grams of crack worth more than \$12,000, an amount that bumped the case up to the federal level. This was Thomas's third strike, and if convicted, he would spend the rest of his life in prison.

Federal prosecutors were preparing the case for trial when our first Tainted Justice story hit. The story prompted them to reexamine what had led up to Thomas's arrest. The facts didn't add up.

In an application for a search warrant, Jeff said Benny had tipped him off to a guy named Pooh Bear who stored guns and sold marijuana and crack from his mother's row house. Jeff claimed that he and another cop watched Benny knock on the door and buy marijuana from Pooh Bear. Jeff described Pooh Bear as tall, about six-two, and thin, roughly 180 pounds.

"I never heard of a guy named Pooh Bear. I never made a buy at this place," Benny told us.

Thomas Cooper never went by the nickname Pooh Bear and wasn't exactly thin—he topped the scale at 350 pounds.

Federal prosecutors decided to drop the charges "in the interests of justice." It was the first case to be dismissed since Barbara and I had started the Tainted Justice series.

I called Cooper's public defender, Nina Carpinello Spizer, who told me she had always been troubled by the case because the warrant gave an inaccurate description and nickname for Cooper.

"We never suspected that this was all made up," she told me. "We didn't know until it came out in the newspaper," she said, referring to our first Tainted Justice story.

Thomas Cooper was set to walk free at any time. We wanted to talk to him, or at least find his relatives and see his house.

When Barbara walked up to his three-story brick row house with smudged cream paint and brown trim, she had a gnawing feeling in the pit of her stomach. The house, owned by the Philadelphia Housing Authority, sat across the street from an elementary school for children pre-K through eighth grade.

It was around 2:30 in the afternoon, and school had just let out. Children clamored outside in their winter coats, and Barbara knew that to get home, these kids had to walk past corner drug boys with dark hoodies pulled tight over their heads to shade their hard-boiled eyes.

Barbara and I knew that nothing tore down a neighborhood faster or harder than drug houses. They attracted desperate addicts who were unpredictable when they couldn't get a fix and potentially dangerous when they did. They took over abandoned houses and made them crack dens or shooting galleries. Many dealers were never far from a weapon and often shot each other over territory or nonsense—it didn't matter. Children, some of them toddlers, had been gunned down in the crossfire, even outside a school. Neighbors feared telling cops about the drug trade on their block, believing their homes would be firebombed.

Barbara knocked on Thomas Cooper's worn front door. Cooper's mother, a woman we'll call Helen, let Barbara into the gloomy, sparse living room, empty except for two chairs. Helen plopped down in one, and Barbara carefully perched herself on a wobbly metal folding chair with a bent, misshapen leg, knowing that with one wrong move, she would topple to the floor.

Helen was forty-nine but looked haggard and moved so precariously, she appeared more like a sickly sixty-year-old. A colostomy bag was attached to her hip. She blamed two recent surgeries on the stress of the raid and the "nasty" cops who threw her son in jail.

Barbara had no doubt that she was sitting in a drug house.

While Helen said she was angry that the cop had set up her son, she made no apologies for Thomas or his lifestyle. Drugs were a cottage industry, the one and only economic engine in her section of town.

Thomas mostly hung out on the third floor, and Helen said she seldom climbed the stairs to see his bedroom or look at what he kept inside. Against the backdrop of a bedroom window that overlooked the elementary school, Thomas cut, weighed, and packaged a potpourri of drugs with studious precision.

Helen told Barbara she suspected that the search warrant was bogus because her son never ran a knock-and-buy operation.

"This is not like you could come to my house, knock on my door, and come in and buy drugs," she said.

Barbara knew that Helen, without saying it, meant that her son didn't roll that way—he gave the drugs to street corner dealers, probably so he wouldn't risk getting his family booted out of public housing. This was home. The family had lived there ten years.

"I don't understand why the cops were here," Helen said with a shrug.

"Did you know your son was selling drugs?" Barbara asked flat-out.

"I kind of thought it, but I didn't see it myself," Helen said.

Some moms of drug dealers played dumb, telling us that they had no idea what cops had found in their homes. Not Helen. She told Barbara she knew cops had discovered crack cocaine, cocaine, and marijuana. She didn't talk specifics or mention that inside her son's bedroom, Jeff and his squad found marijuana in eighty-nine glass jars with pink lids and a digital scale.

Thomas didn't have a job because of a bad knee, yet police found almost $2,000 in his pocket when he was arrested.

"They tore the whole house up. They didn't find no guns," she proclaimed, punctuating the end of her sentence with a slight smile and an expectant pause, as if waiting for Barbara to respond, "You go, girl! Those pesky cops are always making a big deal out of nothing."

Helen cast herself in the role of victim. "It really makes me angry," she said. "Cops are supposed to help us, not to lock people up for nothing so they can make themselves feel better. I think they get off on making themselves feel better."

Barbara emerged from the house feeling like a hypocrite. She never intended to become a champion for the city's drug dealers. It's one thing to get all high and mighty about cops who piss all over the US Constitution, but she didn't have to live here. Her children never had to go to school across the street from a drug dealer's house.

Barbara could parachute into the city's blood-splattered neighborhoods to report on the latest murder, then go home to comfy suburbia, where she never awoke to the sound of gunfire at midnight.

On the first morning of Thomas's freedom, Barbara and I had a front-page story about how Pooh Bear was released from prison because the search warrant seemed to rely on fabricated evidence. The headline on the story: "Dismissed! People Paper Exposé Leads to Release of North Philly Man."

Barbara and I groaned when we saw the photo and headline. We knew that the average reader would take one look at the headline and conclude that we were gleeful that we had helped free the neighborhood crack vendor. Most readers don't know that reporters don't write headlines. To further make us appear that we were empathetic to Cooper's plight, the story featured a family photo of Thomas, this happy hulk of a man, grinning from ear to ear while holding his two small nephews, ages two and four months. The timing couldn't be worse.

The day the story ran, yet one more slain police officer was buried. This time it was John Pawlowski, just twenty-five years old, the fifth officer killed in the line of duty in the past twelve months.

It was a hellish period for a police department that felt under siege. In a city where cops were heroes, the number of police deaths in such a short span was unprecedented. Soccer moms displayed photos of fallen officers in the back windows of their minivans. Cops fastened black ribbons over their badges, and working-class guys with grease under their nails wore T-shirts or buttons to memorialize the latest fallen cop.

For each funeral, the city came to a virtual standstill to allow for the motorcades that stretched for miles. Thousands of mourners, some waving American flags, lined the streets outside the Cathedral Basilica of Saints Peter and Paul. Cops from as far away as Canada came to pay their respects. The sound of sobs, the wail of bagpipes, and the *tat-boom-tat* of drums rose from the crowd as each flag-draped coffin was loaded into the hearse.

Pawlowski, whose father and brother were also cops, was shot to death by a revolving-door criminal, a parolee with a decade-long arrest record for theft, robbery, and gun crimes. When Pawlowski responded to a 911 call from a cabbie who said Scruggs was threatening him, Pawlowski ordered Scruggs to raise his hands. Instead, Scruggs squeezed the trigger of a .357 Magnum that had been tucked inside his coat pocket. A bullet tore into Pawlowski's upper chest, just over the top of his bulletproof vest.

Police Commissioner Ramsey and Mayor Nutter spoke at Pawlowski's funeral, where the cries of Pawlowski's wife, Kimmy, his childhood sweetheart, echoed through the cavernous cathedral. Kimmy was five months pregnant with their first child, a son she would name after her husband. A grainy ultrasound photo was tucked into Pawlowski's folded hands before undertakers closed his brushed copper casket.

To some readers, Barbara and I were no better than killers like Scruggs. "It's people like you who are to blame for the unprecedented violence against the Philadelphia Police," one e-mailed us.

Barbara and I were targeted on Domelights.com, an Internet forum where cops, their supporters, and cop wannabes vented anonymously. The website's slogan—"The Voice of the Good Guys"—was a joke. Many of the postings were angry, racist rants. In one posting, the writer described black children as "a bunch of ghetto monkey faces." Cops and others who posted on the site dubbed us "Slime Sistas," some wished us dead, and a few wrote that they hoped we got raped and no one would respond when we called 911. I didn't tell Karl that cops had posted our home address on the site.

The verbal assault became so savage that our colleague Jill Porter felt compelled to write a column defending us. "You may be furious that a suspected drug dealer was freed—as well you should be. But don't aim your fury at Laker and Ruderman," she wrote.

Again and again, our critics argued, Who cares if cops cut corners or lie to take a drug dealer off the street? They believed that the ends justified the means.

The argument reminded Barbara and me of a famous scene from the 1992 movie *A Few Good Men*, a courtroom drama about two US Marines on trial for killing a fellow marine. When pressed by the prosecutor for the truth about the murder, Colonel Nathan Jessup, played by Jack Nicholson, barks, "You can't handle the truth!" meaning that national security comes at a price. "Son, we live in a world that has walls. And those walls have to be guarded by men with guns. Who's gonna do it? You?"

Yes, Barbara and I weren't cops. We didn't know how it felt to chase down an armed robber or deranged killer, only to find ourselves in a dark alley, staring into the barrel of a gun. But we did know that when reporters fabricated stories, when they invented people, facts, or quotes, they tarnished the entire industry and eroded trust. The same applied to cops, only more so. Martin Luther King Jr. put it this way: "Injustice anywhere is a threat to justice everywhere."

12

BARBARA AND I WERE HUDDLED OVER
MY COMPUTER WRITING OUR NEXT
TAINTED JUSTICE STORY. THE NEWS-
ROOM WAS UNUSUALLY LIVELY FOR
a Sunday evening. It was Oscar night, and
editors had ordered pizza, as they did for
all big events—election night, the Super
Bowl, the World Series. Reporters and copy
editors gathered, vulture-like, around a
white cardboard tower of pizza boxes. They
pulled apart the gooey slices, wiped their
greasy fingers on thin takeout napkins—or
on their jeans—and then zipped back to
their desks.

From my desk, I could see the Sunday-
night editor, Will Bunch, furiously typing
away at his computer behind stacks of yellowed newspapers. Will, the Ivy League–
educated, fifty-year-old mad scientist of
the *Daily News*, always looked like he'd just
jammed a metal fork into an electric outlet,
with his thin strands of hair zigzagging every

which way. Between bites of pizza, Will took generous swigs of Diet Coke straight from the two-liter bottle. By night's end, the bottle would be empty, left on a desk smeared with sticky brown crop circles of corn syrup and a dusting of dandruff.

Will, like everyone else in the newsroom, had just learned that the parent company of the *Daily News* and *Inquirer* had filed for Chapter 11 bankruptcy protection. As he worked on a piece about the filing, which he later posted on his liberal-infused blog *Attytood*, reporters began to Google "Chapter 11" to see if they'd still get paid.

Barbara and I barely looked up, deaf to the chatter of doom around us. We had come in on our day off to write a story about a woman named Lady Gonzalez. Gar, our editor, wanted the story for Monday's front cover. We could hear the thundering hooves of *Inquirer* reporters behind us, and we were determined to outrun them. That meant working double-time to get our story in the paper.

We'd spent most of the week chasing tips that Jeff wasn't the only blemished cop in his squad. A suburban narcotics cop who occasionally joined forces with Philly drug cops called Barbara with a tip that one cop in Jeff's squad was known as the Boob Man.

"Boob Man?"

"Yeah. You know. He fondles women. He's a perv. He goes up under their shirts and touches their breasts when he's on a raid," he told Barbara.

"Oh my God. You've got to be kidding me," Barbara said.

"I'm not fucking with you. He gets them alone in a room. All the other cops know it. I hear he likes large-breasted women—the bigger, the better."

Around the same time, I'd heard similar rumblings from Benny. It wasn't long before we discovered that the cop with the breast fetish wasn't an urban myth. In hunting down people who had been set up by Jeff, we met Lady Gonzalez, a soft-spoken, almost demure woman with almond-shaped brown eyes, smooth skin, high cheekbones, Angelina Jolie lips, and a small diamond stud in her nose. Her father named her Lady because he thought his tiny, delicate baby was deserving of such a regal name.

We met Lady on a Friday night in her tidy home with burgundy walls, CDs stacked in towers inside wood cabinets, comfy sofas, and family photos pinned to the fridge with magnets. She stood only five feet and had a curvy figure and a shy smile. Barbara and I could tell immediately from the moment we met her that she was not just skittish; she was frightened. She fiddled with the dark hair that swept over her shoulders and massaged her hands in an obsessive-compulsive way, and her sentences periodically drifted off as she tried to compose herself.

Jeff and his squad had raided this house where she lived with her husband, Albert Nunez, and her five young children. Jeff had written in a search warrant that Albert had sold a packet of cocaine to Benny, but Benny told us that was a lie—he'd never bought drugs from Albert.

When Jeff and eight other cops burst through the front door, Lady was home with the children. When Lady saw Jeff point a drawn gun at her, she froze. One cop took her children, crying and screaming, to a neighbor's house. While the other cops ripped the house apart in search of drugs, one cop, whom Lady described as husky and average height, led her into a small room off the kitchen.

Lady recounted how the barrel-bellied cop shifted his body, shuffling his feet closer to hers. She tried to back up, but there was nowhere to go. The wall was at her back.

"He asked me if I had any tattoos. I told him I had one on

my lower back," Lady told us. "He told me to show it to him. He pushed down my jeans so he could see the crack of my ass and where I have a tattoo of the Puerto Rican flag," she said, illustrating how low he pulled down her pants.

"Mmmm, a Puerto Rican," he said.

He spun her around, unzipped her blue jacket, hiked up her shirt and bra, and fondled her breasts.

"I was so scared," Lady told us, her voice shaking as she wiped a tear from the corner of her eye. "I was in a panic. I thought he was going to rape me."

The cop stopped and stepped away from Lady only when he heard the other cops stomp down the staircase and head toward the kitchen. At first, the cops found nothing more than Albert's dime bag of weed, but during one last sweep, Jeff emerged from the back room with a teddy bear with a small pouch secreted inside. The pouch contained forty-seven packets of cocaine. Albert claimed the drugs were planted. Maybe. Maybe not.

What shook up Lady most was that the cop who sexually assaulted her had then pocketed her house key and had warned that he'd be back. He promised that he'd return every day, every night. The night we met Lady, more than a year had passed since the cop had fondled her. He hadn't been back, but Lady couldn't get his face out of her head.

"I think of him. I dream of him," she told us. "Still, till this day, I think he's going to come back."

She hadn't reported the incident to internal affairs because she didn't think they'd believe her, and they might even retaliate.

"I'm sorry, but why am I going to report this to a police officer when a police officer stood in front of me and molested me?" she asked us.

She agreed to talk to Barbara and me only because she suspected she wasn't the first victim, and probably not the last.

We believed she was right.

In the story, we didn't identify the cop who fondled Lady by name. We didn't have the goods. Not yet.

Barbara and I finished writing our Lady story and were about to power down our computers when, at 11:38 p.m., Brian Tierney, our company's charismatic CEO, issued a staffwide call to arms. The e-mail subject line read, "Important Notice." It should have read, "Don't Panic."

"As a company, we have been hit with a perfect storm, including a dramatic decline in total revenue, the worst economic conditions since the Great Depression and a debt structure which is out of line with current economic reality," Tierney wrote. "Now more than ever, we need to continue the hard work that has already begun."

The company's bankruptcy filing was the number-three story on CNN, right after North Korea's suspected missile tests and President Obama's stimulus plan.

The *Daily News* and *Inquirer* were officially part of the Chapter 11 Club, joining the ranks of other major dailies on death watch. The *Los Angeles Times*, the *Chicago Tribune*, the *Minneapolis Star Tribune*, the *Baltimore Sun*, and the Journal Register Company, which owned twenty-two daily newspapers and three hundred nondaily publications—all were in bankruptcy protection.

The Big Fall for the *Daily News* and *Inquirer* had taken only three years. In 2006 Tierney had spearheaded a group of Philadelphia-area investors who purchased the *Daily News*, the *Inquirer*, and our website, Philly.com, for $562 million, which included pension liabilities. Tierney, a flamboyant advertising and public relations executive who put up $10 million of his own money, was supposed to be our savior, the hometown guy who freed us from "the cold dead hand of Knight Ridder," as *Inky* Metro columnist Tom Ferrick Jr. put it. Over the years, the publicly traded Knight Ridder Inc. had decimated our newsrooms with its slash-and-burn cost-cutting. Private local ownership was supposed to be the antidote to Wall Street's iron-fisted demands for high profit margins.

Tierney was a much-needed shot of energy and determination. He dreamed about flying. He really believed he could revive local and national advertising, reverse circulation losses, and beat back competition from the Internet.

We were leery at first. Tierney had been an archenemy of Philadelphia reporters for years. He was known for intimidating and browbeating reporters in defense of his clients. If he hated a story, he was quick to call editors and complain, railing that the reporters were biased, unethical, and incompetent.

Tierney grew up learning to fight for what he wanted. The fourth of five brothers, he spent his early childhood in a largely blue-collar Philly suburb, where his mom was a waitress and his father was a claims adjuster. He sucked his naysayers up with a straw and spat them out. He thrived on challenge, especially if the stakes were high. Philly was Tierney's home, and he fit perfectly in this town of scrappers.

Philadelphians were the stars of not one but two reality television shows: A&E TV's *Parking Wars*, which featured ticket writers and car booters in confrontations with Philly loudmouths; and the Discovery Channel's *Wreck Chasers*, in which the city is billed as "the Wild West of tow-trucking." Television producers needed only to roll the cameras, and they were guaranteed drama.

Philadelphia sports fans were famously obnoxious and

rowdy. Their notoriety could be traced all the way back to a December day in 1968 when the Eagles played horribly and fans booed Santa Claus, pelting the red-suited Saint Nick with snowballs during the game's halftime show. For a time, Lincoln Financial Field was the only NFL stadium in the country that housed a jail with four holding cells, for unruly Eagles fans.

Tierney was a gloves-off brawler, and he wouldn't have wanted to be a newspaper publisher in any other city. When he bought the *Inquirer* and *Daily News*, Tierney had put everything on the line—not only his personal wealth but his reputation. Tierney understood the importance of image and had an ego large enough to power every house in Philly. He wanted to go down in Philadelphia history as the local guy who single-handedly saved the city's newspapers.

In a sense, Tierney was our best hope. We knew to fail meant that Tierney had failed, and that wasn't how Tierney wanted the story written.

Tierney's caffeinated enthusiasm was infectious. On his first day on the job, Tierney gave a champagne send-off to a fleet of delivery trucks adorned with the company's new slogan: "Bringing Home the News." He danced at a pep rally, brought in Eagles cheerleaders, and boldly declared, "The next great era of Philadelphia journalism begins today."

I had learned I was going to be laid off from the *Inquirer* four months after Tierney took the helm. Suddenly, Tierney-land didn't seem so magical.

Tierney blamed the cuts on a "permanent" free fall in ad revenues. Classified advertising, too, took a beating, as ads for jobs, real estate, cars, pets, and personals migrated to Craigslist and other Internet sites. At the same time, newspaper circulation was in decline. We had trained a whole generation of readers to get their news for free on the Internet while drinking $4 lattes. Not even the smartest people in our industry could figure out how to close the Pandora's box that we had opened.

Tierney's group had overpaid for the papers, borrowed too much money, and now struggled to make debt payments. As they scrounged around for $20 million in savings, they discussed laying off as many as 150 of the 415 *Inquirer* newsroom jobs. Reporters who had worked at the *Inquirer* for almost a decade were in danger of losing their jobs. I had only been there four years. And I was number eleven on the *Inquirer* layoff list.

"Tierney should change the company's slogan to 'Bringing Home the Pink Slip,' " Karl snorted when I called home.

I tried to focus on work, but my bosses kept coming over to my desk. "Why aren't you looking for a job?" they'd ask. A huge swath of reporters—myself included—began to spend our workday writing cover letters and tweaking résumés.

I soon landed a job offer from the *New York Daily News*, but I wanted the *Inquirer* to lay me off so I could collect my severance. Bill Marimow, the *Inky* editor, was in his office when I got back from my interview in Manhattan. I summoned the balls to ask if he could finagle my severance pay, even though I'd be gone before the layoffs hit.

Marimow was an old-fashioned newspaper man. He'd circulate through the newsroom, shirtsleeves rolled up to the elbows. An avuncular champion of his reporters, especially those who hustled, he emitted a quiet strength. "And how are you today, Miss Ruderman," he'd say slowly, enunciating each word. When I told Marimow that I'd gotten a job at the *New York Daily News*, this soft-spoken, two-time Pulitzer winner sat back in his chair and smiled.

"I didn't know you'd be willing to work at a . . . tabloid,"
Marimow said. "Let me make a call."

The next day at work, I answered my phone to find Tierney
on the other end. "Congratulations on your new job at *Philadelphia Daily News*," he said. I was saved.

On January 3, 2007, my first day at the *Daily News*, Tierney
sent layoff notices to seventy-one *Inquirer* employees. I envisioned tears, anger, and despair two floors above in the *Inquirer* newsroom. "The guillotine has finally fallen," said one
Inky reporter who got laid off. I had survivor's guilt.

But two years had passed, and now I was at the *Daily News*
working on Tainted Justice, and the guilt had subsided—
even vanished. Barbara and I were deep into the series, even
though we knew that our industry, on journalistic hospice,
appeared to be nearing the end, taking its last few labored
breaths. Newspapers had become "quaint," like the milkman
or the paperboy.

So on that Sunday night, when Barbara and I wrapped up
the Lady story, we were relieved the paper was still alive, albeit
barely.

At 11:00 p.m. or so, we walked out of the newsroom, tense,
tired, hungry. Barbara turned to me.

"What if the paper closes before we've finished the Tainted
Justice series?" she asked.

13

"YOU AND WENDY NEED TO BE CARE-
FUL," A COP SOURCE WARNED BARBARA
DURING A CONVERSATION FROM HIS
PERSONAL CELL. "THE STUFF YOU GUYS
are reporting is serious. A lot's at stake.
Cops could go down 'cause of this."

On top of the hate e-mails, Barbara and I
had started to get nasty voice-mail messages
and hang-up calls. The paper's top editor,
Michael Days, was concerned enough to ask
the company's telecommunications staff to
trace the calls. Denise Gallo, the scarily efficient *Daily News* den mom who served as
Michael's right arm, came over to us with a
printout of incoming calls to the newsroom.
She highlighted calls to our extensions in
yellow. "Girls, do you recognize any of these
numbers?" At fifty-seven, Denise always referred to us as the Girls, though Barbara was
fifty-one and I was thirty-nine. No number
looked familiar, except for one—a hang-up
from my home phone. Karl had a habit of

calling and hanging up when I didn't answer. The three of us erupted in giggles.

We tried to brush off the anger directed at us, but our imaginations sometimes led to our brains' dark crannies. I was afraid to get my morning newspaper. I'd open the front door and scan up and down my street before dashing to the lawn to snatch the paper. I'd quickly dead-bolt the door behind me.

"Why do you keep locking the door?" Karl asked after dropping Brody at school.

"I don't know," I said dumbly.

I wasn't a door-locker by nature, and Karl knew that I rarely bothered to lock the door when we left to go grocery shopping or out to dinner.

During a morning run, on a winding road without side-walks, Barbara jumped into the bushes when a speeding pickup truck veered toward her. This is it, she thought. The pickup rocketed by, disappearing around a curve, and she breathed puffs of relief, uncertain whether to laugh at herself or hurry home.

Barbara's neighbor, Hutch, walked across the street to her house every night before she came home from work to flip on every overhead light and lamp. The past three years, Barbara and Hutch had had an on-again, off-again relationship. She'd met him three months after moving here with her teen-age children, her divorce still raw. She gardened obsessively, thinking a manicured lawn, prettied up with flowers, could mask the chaos of an uprooted life. On a Saturday afternoon in May, Barbara kneeled in the dirt and planted yellow and purple pansies. She thought of her ex-husband, all the week-end afternoons, twenty-five years together, spent working on the lawn. She looked a mess in her mud-splotched running clothes, her eyes pink and puffy from crying, when Hutch yelled from across the street, "How about coming over for a get-to-know-your-neighbor drink?"

It took her three weeks to fall for him.

Hutch, a rugged, broad-shouldered, six-foot-tall man with a strong jaw, was like a teenager with a bad-boy edge. He had a bald spot and a nose that sported a bump and curved slightly to the right—the result of three bloody breaks sustained in ice hockey and wrestling dustups. He didn't walk; he swaggered, exuding self-confidence.

After the divorce, Barbara probably needed someone like Hutch. They spent evenings in his basement, dancing to Led Zeppelin and the Cure like high-schoolers. He wasn't guarded with his emotions and spoke without a filter. But over time, some of his raunchy, off-color remarks made Barbara cringe. They often had spats about race, politics, priorities, lifestyles, children. A gun lover, he kept a 9mm Glock in his bedroom dresser and stashed shotguns and hunting rifles in a locked safe. Barbara hated guns. The highs of the relationship were euphoric; the lows chipped away at her.

Barbara hadn't dated in over twenty-five years, and Hutch was the opposite of her ex-husband, Matt. Matt was reserved, reliable, predictable, and so steady that his emotional pendulum rarely budged. Those were some reasons she fell in love with him. He grounded her. Matt was the "Whoooa, Nellie" to her exuberant "Giddy up! Woo-hoo!"

The problem was, Hutch was a little too "Woo-hoo" and that scared Barbara. She pictured herself with a man whose personality was a blend of Matt and Hutch's. But dating was hell.

On one date, a guy pulled up his pant leg to show Barbara

his tattoos. On his calf, he had tattooed the name of his then-wife inside a heart. When he started dating after his divorce, his new girlfriend hated the tattoo, so he covered up his ex-wife's name with a rose and added the girlfriend's name in bigger print underneath. Barbara imagined her name, in even larger letters, scrawled underneath the ex-girlfriend's name, camouflaged with a giant pink chrysanthemum.

Another guy described himself as "athletic and toned" on his Match.com profile and looked about 180 pounds in his photo. Barbara didn't recognize him when they met. Somewhere along the way, he'd packed on an extra hundred pounds. He confessed that he first called Barbara from the family station wagon because he was still living with his ex-wife. He assured Barbara that he wasn't intimate with his ex and slept in the den on a broken La-Z-Boy chair.

Still another guy, who Barbara had really liked, turned out to be a pathological liar. He even spun a tale about making pot roast for his grown daughters, when he'd really ordered pizza.

"It was the pot roast," Barbara told me incredulously. "Why would he lie about pot roast? I mean, pot roast, Wendy. As if I care that he didn't cook."

Barbara shared her dating horror stories with Hutch. He had a few of his own.

"I keep telling you. I'm the one for you," said Hutch, who then smiled, threw his shoulders back, and swept his hands up and down his body, stopping at his crotch. "Look. I'm the full package."

Hutch liked to parody the line from *Jerry Maguire*, in which Tom Cruise tells Renée Zellweger, "You complete me."

"I," Hutch said with a theatrical pause, "complete myself."

Even when Barbara and Hutch weren't dating, they stayed

friends, and Hutch loved being her protector. After he lit up her house like the Griswold family's Christmas, he would poke his head into every closet and under all three beds. During the nightly patrol, he had a Glock holstered on his hip, just in case. Years ago, he'd been a cop and had a license to carry.

"Hutch can be soooo sweet sometimes," Barbara told me.

Around this time, George Bochetto, the hawkish attorney hired by Jeff, was readying a Laker-Ruderman smackdown. He assured Jeff that we were easy prey. He'd clobber us. On Jeff's dime, Bochetto hired a private investigator to blast holes in Benny's story and discredit our work.

The PI spent days interviewing Benny's relatives and former bosses, who characterized Benny as an unredeemable liar, con artist, drug addict, and thief, disowned by his own father. He pulled Benny's criminal record and interviewed cops who vouched for Jeff, casting him as the kind of cop they'd want beside them in a foxhole. Jeff's former partner, Richard Eberhart, denied knowing that Jeff rented a house to Benny. He claimed Barbara had twisted his words. The PI pulled Jeff's awards, commendations, and letters of praise from community leaders. He compiled the interviews and documents into a textbook-thick binder, which included exhibits A through K.

With the PI's report in hand, Bochetto set about organizing a news conference with the Fraternal Order of Police. In Philly, politicians tiptoed around the FOP. Lawmakers and judges who dared to poke the 14,600-member beehive with a stick felt their collective sting. The FOP relentlessly bashed municipal court judge Craig Washington when he refused to allow a memorial photo of slain officer John Pawlowski to rest on the bench during court proceedings. The police union hung a huge banner reading "DUMP Judge Craig Washington" outside its headquarters.

Barbara and I had whacked the beehive with a baseball bat. We'd taken on one of their own, and the cops were about to unite in a swarm.

14

WE WALKED OVER TO FOP HEADQUAR-
TERS ON A FRIGID, WIND-WHIPPED AF-
TERNOON IN LATE FEBRUARY. A UNION
SECRETARY DIRECTED US TO A HALL,
no fancier than a grade school gymna-
sium, where the FOP held parties and fund-
raisers for families of fallen officers. Rows of
folding chairs sat before a stage. Reporters
from every news outlet in the city filed in.
Barbara and I took seats up front. We exchanged polite, nervous chatter with the
Inky reporter seated next to us. FOP president John McNesby took to the podium. A
semicircle of fifteen plainclothes cops lined
up behind McNesby. They stood shoulder to
shoulder, arms crossed, glaring at us.

Bring it on, I thought.

"At a time when we're burying police officers at an alarming rate," McNesby began,
"we have a newspaper that on the same day—
the same day—we're laying one of our fallen
heroes to rest, is persecuting another officer
for frivolous, mindless, baseless allegations."

McNesby was a former narcotics cop who had worked with Jeff. With his square head, rotund body, and triple-thick turkey neck, McNesby was a city icon. He was famous for his inappropriate, politically incorrect rants, which reporters considered a gift, a pinch of hot sauce to spice up an otherwise bland story.

McNesby swore that the FOP would "go to the wall" to defend Jeff. The attack turned personal. "You have to remember, you're dealing with a confidential informant here. A confidential informant in the city of Philadelphia is one step above a *Daily News* reporter."

The snarky remark drew laughter and applause from the roomful of cops. I could feel my cheeks redden in anger. I crossed my legs and began to furiously pump my foot. I was having a Napoleonic moment. I envisioned pulling all of McNesby's search warrants. He better watch it, or we'll investigate his fat ass, I thought.

Next came Bochetto's turn on the podium. He handed out copies of the binder compiled by his private investigator. The binder, Bochetto promised, offered proof that Jeff had rented the house to Sonia, not Benny. How was Jeff to know that Benny had struck up a romantic relationship with Sonia? The argument was so stupid that I bit the inside of my cheek to stifle a snicker.

The supremely confident Bochetto was spooling out a barn burner. He began to pontificate: Naturally Benny was scared. The guy set up scores of dangerous drug dealers who wouldn't hesitate to kill him. "His life was in danger and in order to save himself, he made up this fanciful story . . . that Jeff Cujdik made up all the facts in the affidavits and that it couldn't possibly be him. Why? To save his own skin!"

Bellowing from the podium with the fire of a preacher,

Bochetto claimed he had warned Barbara and me, weeks ago, that to print Jeff's name would put the cop and his family in danger, and we'd responded, "That's not our concern." It was like pouring gasoline on a flame; a disapproving gasp rippled from one cop to the next. I wanted to jump out of my seat and scream, as if it were the Salem witch trials, "He's lying!"

Bochetto said he'd been preparing a lawsuit against the *Daily News* when the company filed for bankruptcy protection. Now he wasn't sure if a suit would be feasible. The press conference, he said, would serve to put an end to the hysteria generated by a newspaper desperate to stave off its extinction.

McNesby and Bochetto vilified us for almost fifty minutes. The moment they finished, TV news crews swung around and trained their video cameras on Barbara and me. They trailed us out of the building; they needed b-roll of our stricken faces for the evening newscast. Two radio reporters and the *Inky*'s Joseph Slobodzian, whom reporters called Joe Slo because they couldn't pronounce his name, asked us for comment. Barbara and I didn't know what to do.

"Maybe you should call Michael Days for comment," I said.

Never before had the FOP orchestrated a press conference specifically to single out and intimidate individual reporters. The attack was unprecedented, and Michael Days, a journalist for more than thirty years, knew it. Looking back, he wished he'd sent another reporter, instead of Barbara and me, and fretted that he'd inadvertently subjected us to a public flogging.

Now he worried about our safety. Police officers were anguished and their emotions volatile over the deaths of so many of their brethren, and Michael feared they'd misplace their anger.

Philly cops and the *Daily News* had a long-standing adversarial relationship. To us, "the People Paper" wasn't just a slogan; it was a journalistic doctrine. That meant we didn't just regurgitate the police version of a controversial story, like a police shooting. We hit the streets to get the neighborhood's account.

Michael knew the Tainted Justice series would forge an even wider divide between the newspaper and the police department. But he didn't waver.

Michael, at fifty-five, had a glossy bald head and a compact, athletic build. He favored steel-gray suits, paired with a bold-colored tie and crisp shirt. He scanned the paper early every morning and tore out stories he liked, scribbling words of praise on Post-it notes. Denise Gallo trotted across the room in her sensible pumps and slipped the Mike-agrams into our mailboxes. Michael was so generous with accolades that sometimes we wanted to ask, Did you really like it? Or are you just being nice?

At news meetings he listened intently, his right palm pressed against his cheek, as editors describe the day's top stories. He never raised his voice. He wasn't the type of boss people feared. When he disapproved of something one of his editors said, he'd drop his chin to his chest and tilt his head to the side. He'd raise his brows and widen his eyes with a fixed stare.

"Oh reeeeally now," he'd say slowly, probably thinking, C'mon, are you for real?

And when something tickled him, he let out a loud, contagious chuckle that made his body shake so hard that he gripped his tie to keep it from swaying back and forth.

Michael became the first black editor in *Daily News* history in 2005. He loved stories that thrust the bullhorn into the hands of the little guys, people on the fringes who felt neglected, even punted to the curb, by the city's power elite. Michael understood the struggles of row-house people because he was one. He and his younger sister grew up in a hard-bitten part of North Philly with their mom, who didn't have a high school diploma and worked long hours making salads at the stately and grand Ben Franklin Hotel.

His mom, a strict, no-nonsense woman who stressed education, wouldn't allow Michael to use the word *can't*. She enrolled him in Catholic school, even though they were Baptists, because she believed public schools weren't good enough. They rarely ate in restaurants, didn't have money for a car, and his mom didn't have one credit card, but once a year, she took them to see Santa Claus at the Wanamaker Building, where they ate lunch in the elegant Crystal Tea Room with hand-carved columns, intricate crystal chandeliers, and crisp table linens.

Michael came of age when the civil rights movement was in full throttle. In 1967 Thurgood Marshall became the first black Supreme Court justice, but out on the streets, police were using tear gas, whips, and clubs to subdue civil rights marchers. Michael was a high school sophomore when Martin Luther King Jr. was assassinated. He boiled with anger.

In 1991 Michael and his wife did something few couples would even consider: they adopted four brothers, between the ages of four and nine, who had bounced from foster home to foster home. The boys had deep emotional scars from being born to a drug-addicted mom and a father they didn't know. Michael and his wife soon learned the youngest was autistic.

At home and at work, Michael dutifully played the role of quiet guardian. Barbara and I never doubted he would defend us. The quote he provided for the FOP story was so Michael—succinct and definitive:

"The stories are accurate and we will defend our reports and our reporters."

15

A FEW DAYS AFTER THE FRATERNAL
ORDER OF POLICE NEWS CONFERENCE,
IN EARLY MARCH 2009, *TIME* MAGAZINE
LISTED THE *DAILY NEWS* AS NUMBER
one on its list of "The 10 Most Endangered
Newspapers in America."

But Barbara and I had a plan that had
nothing to do with our newspaper's pre-
dicted demise. We had to track down every
drug informant who had ever worked
with Jeff. High on our list was Tiffany, a
hellcat and former stripper from the row-
house-lined streets of Philly's Kensington
neighborhood, home to a hodgepodge of
hustlers, from hookers and drug dealers to
minimum-wage workers juggling two jobs
and sorry souls eternally on the dole.

Tiffany's ex-boyfriend claimed that she
and Jeff had conspired to set him up in a
lover's revenge plot, and that Jeff lied on the
search warrant used to raid his house.

We wanted to hear what Tiffany had to

say about Jeff. We knew she wouldn't be happy to see us. But it never—not for a minute—occurred to us that it could be dangerous for us to pursue Tiffany, even though a year earlier, cops had arrested her for bashing a man in the head with a glass bottle and stealing $250 and a necklace.

On a cold gray afternoon in early March, with a snowstorm looming, Barbara knocked on the door at Tiffany's two-story redbrick row house. At twenty-eight, Tiffany was the mother of two kids by two different men and still lived with her parents. Her mom, Mickey, answered the door with a Marlboro Menthol wedged between two fingers. Mickey stood steely and stone-faced in the doorway. Barbara offered a sunny hello and thrust out her hand, which Mickey reluctantly shook. Still gripping Mickey's palm, Barbara stepped closer and wormed her way into the living room.

Mickey was a stout and sturdy woman who favored baggy T-shirts and sweats. She was fifty-one years old and had had the same job as a machine operator at a ribbon factory for nearly two decades, working the overnight shift from 2:30 a.m. to 1:00 p.m. On Fridays, she stopped by the liquor store to pick up her favorite—coconut vodka.

Barbara smiled as she plopped herself down on a velour couch the color of rotted red grapes and opened her notebook.

"I was just wondering," said Barbara, trying to sound casual. "Have you ever seen Jeff? Has he ever been over to the house?"

Mickey proceeded to tell Barbara that Jeff had showed up on her doorstep after Tiffany got arrested for aggravated assault and robbery. He handed her $300 in cash to bail Tiffany out of jail. Wow, this is good stuff, Barbara thought as she felt the first pinpricks of adrenaline, the rush that reporters feel when they get a juicy nugget. Barbara instinctively knew that Jeff had crossed the line when he footed Tiffany's bail. With her cheeks warm and head down, Barbara scribbled away. She flipped the blue-lined pages with her fingertips like paper somersaults as quickly as Mickey spoke. She was so focused and excited that she didn't pay any attention to the loud stomps from the top of the staircase leading to the second floor. Tiffany barreled down the steps, a she-devil with a pierced nose and long, dirty blond hair flaring out behind her, and charged toward Barbara.

"I'm gonna fuckin' kill you!"

When Barbara looked up, Tiffany loomed over her. The first strike came hard and fast, Tiffany's open hand slamming into Barbara's left cheek and knocking her head sideways. The second belt, to Barbara's right cheek, had even more force. Barbara felt the sting of something hard, maybe Tiffany's rings as they whacked into her cheekbone. Barbara let go of her notebook and crossed her arms over her head in an X shape to shield her face from more blows. Tiffany snatched the notebook and hurled it across the room. It landed near Mickey, who just sat there, on an adjacent couch, not saying a word, as Barbara cried out, "Please! No!"

Barbara stood up, the pen on her lap dropping to the floor, and quickly grabbed her brown leather purse. She crouched low, her back hunched, and darted across the room as if dodging gunfire. Her hand shook as she scooped up the notebook and sprinted out the front door.

As she ran, Barbara fished around in her bottomless, sack-like purse for her cell phone. She flipped open the phone and pressed my number. Her voice was a high-pitched squeak.

"Wendy! Wendy! She hit me!"

I was seated at my desk. I bolted up out of my chair and shouted, "What? What happened?" The reporters who sat near me looked up from their computers. The phone went dead. I dialed her back. No answer. I dialed and redialed, each time getting her voice mail. I began to panic.

Barbara, cheeks aflame, closed her phone when she heard fast footsteps behind her. Barbara glanced over her shoulder and saw Tiffany, a wild-eyed, fuel-raged bullet train, screaming bloody murder into a cell phone.

Tiffany had frantically called Jeff. At that moment, Jeff felt sick: he knew Barbara and I weren't going to stop with just Benny; we planned to track down all of his informants.

In a panic, Barbara finally found her car keys. She struggled to steady her hand as she unlocked the car door, jumped in, locked all the doors, and sped off. When she got a few blocks away, she pulled over and examined her face in the rearview mirror. She wanted to make sure she wasn't bleeding. Then she called me back.

"Tiffany hit me. Twice. Across the face. She threatened to kill me," Barbara said. "But don't worry, I got the notebook . . . but I lost . . . my pen."

It wasn't funny at the time but later, the lost pen would become a running joke between us. The *Daily News* supply closet only stocked cheap Bics, which tended to leak and smudge, so Barbara bought her own special ones: Paper Mate Profile retractable ballpoint pens in assorted colors in packs of four for $3.99 at the grocery store. To her, losing a pen was a big deal.

Barbara knew the city well, having been a Philly reporter for sixteen years, but this, her first assault, rattled her. Suddenly she couldn't figure out how to get back to the office. She asked me to stay on the phone until she found I-95 South, heading toward Center City.

By the time Barbara walked into the newsroom, Brian

Tierney had gathered the staff for a big announcement. Barbara joined the circle of about forty reporters, photographers,
and editors gathered around Tierney near the sports desk.
Because Tierney had filed for Chapter 11 bankruptcy protection just a week ago, the staff was extra jittery and abuzz with
rumors that Tierney planned to merge our ragtag ranks with
the restrained *Inquirer* staff and close the *Daily News*.

We'd been on journalism's endangered species list for decades, and a lot of the old-timers had become numb to death
threats, like prisoners of war. They put out the paper each day
with an attitude that said, *Either shoot me in the head or get out of
my way.*

Tierney nervously swooped back his thick mane of chest-
nut hair, a cross between Donald Trump's and Shaun Cassi-
dy's locks, and explained that starting March 30, the phrase
"an edition of the *Philadelphia Inquirer*" would appear under
the *Daily News* logo on the paper's front page. He assured us
that the two papers would remain intact, with separate news
staffs, and that the move was purely economic. Tierney hoped
that making the two papers a single entity with combined
circulation numbers would help boost ad sales, and save us
money as a single subscriber to wire services.

"Instead of telling advertisers we have 330,000 circulation
(at the *Inquirer*) plus the *Daily News*, it will help to say we have
440,000 daily circulation," Tierney explained to a roomful of
journalists trained to expose and rail against any cooking of
the books in city government who were suddenly resigned to
accepting our own creative math.

But I barely heard what Tierney was saying. I kept looking
at Barbara, who stood among the crowd, somewhat dazed,
gingerly touching her cheeks, which sported angry red slap
marks. I could actually see handprints parallel to her pearl

earrings. She looked dainty in those earrings, with a long strand of fake pearls draped over a peach-and-cream-colored J.Crew sweater. What kind of person would hit Barbara Laker?

I could feel a nervous giggle creeping up my throat. My reaction was inappropriate and insensitive, but I couldn't help it. I kept thinking: What the fuck? Tiffany hauled off on Betty Crocker! It was funny in a horrible kind of way.

"You okay?" I asked after the meeting.

"Do you think it will bruise?" she said.

"I'm gonna get you ice for your face."

When I got back from the cafeteria with Styrofoam cups packed with ice, Barbara was talking to Gar, our editor, who wanted her to press criminal charges.

"If you get killed, it's a good one-day story, but long-term, it's bad for business," I overheard Gar telling Barbara.

She refused to file a police complaint against Tiffany, mostly because she didn't want to become part of the story.

The thing was, Tiffany came from a seamy world, one in which she could, if she wanted, find some lowlife to off Barbara for a price. And Jeff now knew that Tiffany had told us one more thing that could get him in trouble. Jeff and Bochetto wanted more than ever to shut us down. Bochetto got the private investigator right on it.

Tiffany soon found herself in a scene straight out of a film noir. She climbed into the gumshoe's Mercedes-Benz, and they sat in the Home Depot parking lot on Aramingo Avenue, a busy commercial artery lined with big-box stores.

Russell Kolins, a private investigator since 1969, was an old hat. With his weathered, pleasant face and classy business suit, Kolins came off as both grizzled and imperial. He was a marine who worked counterintelligence in Vietnam, and the former owner of a Jersey nightclub called Private Eyes.

The impeccably dressed Kolins began to pepper Tiffany with questions. What did the reporter ask? And what did Tiffany's mom tell her? He needed details, specifically any minefields surrounding Jeff.

Tiffany was spooked. In the mind of this hardened hood diva, Kolins was the embodiment of the Man. He might as well have been a state senator, judge, bank president, corporate CEO. It didn't matter. She had to get out of that car.

Once home, Tiffany wondered what the hell she'd gotten herself into. She called Barbara.

"I'm real sorry I hit you," Tiffany said.

"Tiffany, that's okay. I know you're sorry. I know you didn't mean it," Barbara replied.

I was standing by Barbara's desk when she picked up the phone. My ears perked up: Tiffany? The notorious bitch slapper? I turned to the reporters and editors around me and stage-whispered, "She's on the phone with Tiffany," woodpeckering my finger above Barbara's head. Everyone came over to eavesdrop.

"Wow, Barbara has a new BFF," joked hipster reporter Stephanie Farr.

Tiffany explained to Barbara that she felt confused. She'd thought Jeff was a good guy. If she got jammed up on a traffic ticket or got collared, Jeff helped her out, often with cash. He talked to her like a buddy, all chatty and warm.

"What's going on, kiddo?" Jeff asked, fishing for neighborhood intel that might lead to his next drug bust.

After talking to Kolins, Tiffany realized that Jeff had slapped her informant number on drug buys she never made. She was scared to venture out of her house. She felt like all the local dealers were giving her an accusatory stare-down.

"They think I'm a snitch," she told Barbara.

The informant job, at least under Jeff, came with perks. Jeff rewarded Tiffany and his other informants with cartons of cigarettes, prepaid phone minutes, candy bars, and snacks.

"Here, get your sugar up," he'd say, tossing Benny a Snickers bar.

Barbara and I didn't really think about where Jeff got the stuff. Until we got a phone call from a Center City lawyer.

16

OUR STORY ABOUT TIFFANY AND HOW JEFF HAD PAID HER BAIL MONEY UNEARTHED ONE MORE EXAMPLE OF HOW JEFF HAD CROSSED THE LINE. A few days later, a Philadelphia attorney, Todd Henry, called me. Todd told me he represented a fifty-three-year-old Jordanian shop owner named Samir.

"You know those cops you're writing about?" Todd asked me. "Well, I have a client whose shop was raided by those cops, and he says they took thousands of dollars from him and other stuff like cigarettes," Todd told me.

My heart started to race.

"And you know what, those cops cut all his video surveillance wires. So what do you think? You want to talk to him?"

Absolutely. "Just tell me when and where," I said.

I darted over to Todd's office later that day. Todd's receptionist showed me into a conference room and shut the door. "He'll be with you in a moment."

I took out my notebook, tape recorder, and a pen, lining them up on the glossy wood table. The anticipation of an interview, especially one that held so much promise, was one of life's teeny pleasures, like that first sip of hot coffee in the morning or the gradual dim of lights at the start of a movie.

Todd came into the room and I shook his hand. I looked behind him, expecting to see Samir.

"I'm sorry. Samir changed his mind," Todd said.

Samir was too scared to talk. He feared retaliation from the cops and didn't want a story in the paper.

I walked the nine blocks back to the *Daily News* office, disheartened and anguished. Maybe if I went to Samir's house, I could convince him to tell his story. Wait. No. That might wig him out. Might be better to show up at his smoke shop. . . .

Barbara and I needed to brainstorm. We got something to eat from Gus and Joan, the Greek couple who operated a lunch truck parked outside our office. Barbara got her usual salad—romaine lettuce, tomatoes, egg, cucumbers, mushrooms, grilled chicken, and absolutely no cheese. I almost always ordered a BLT. Back at my desk, I opened a mayo packet with my teeth and squeezed creamy ribbons onto the bread.

"Wendy, I'm telling you this as your friend, if you don't eat more green leafy vegetables, you could get cancer," she said.

"I don't like salad. It's like eating grass." We'd had this conversation a zillion times.

As much as we were the same, Barbara and I were different. She was a frugal, coupon-clipping, to-the-penny bookkeeper; I never looked at my pay stubs and only learned how much money was in my checking account when I withdrew cash from an ATM and looked at the receipt. For breakfast, Barbara ate low-fat Greek yogurt, mixed with fresh berries and raw oatmeal; I ate a chocolate chip muffin. When Barbara's lower back ached, she did core-strengthening exercises; I popped two Aleve. She religiously got an oil change every 3,000 miles; I rarely checked my oil. Barbara obsessed over her throw pillows, which she meticulously arranged on couches and beds in a complex puzzle of patterns and colors; I never bothered to make the bed each morning. I didn't see the point.

Barbara stabbed a plastic fork into her salad, and I wiped grease and mayonnaise from the corners of my mouth with a napkin. We sat in silence, chewing. Then Barbara thought of something. "Wendy, what if there are more Samirs out there?" We remembered from combing through search warrants that Jeff's squad had raided a lot of corner stores. We didn't think much of it at the time, but now we wondered aloud why this elite narcotics squad had zeroed in on so many mom-and-pop stores.

The next morning, Barbara and I headed back to the search warrant room to pull every store raid done by Jeff's squad. We practically jogged to the criminal courthouse, and in a gust of excitement, we flew through the room's doorway—and then came to an abrupt halt, as if we'd careened into a concrete barrier. Two *Inky* reporters and an intern, perched on metal chairs, looked up at us. We exchanged polite yet leery hellos. They were methodically sifting through the onionskin-thin warrants. Barbara and I tried to appear unruffled and blasé, but on the inside, we seethed like territorial hornets. This was OUR secret chamber of buried treasures and it was being invaded by a battalion of *Inky* reporters.

We had learned about the search warrant room through

an attorney source, and for the first few stories about Jeff, Barbara and I had the place to ourselves. Not anymore.

There sat Andy Maykuth, a former foreign correspondent first dispatched to Nicaragua in 1985 and later sent to forty-eight other countries, mostly war-ravaged and dangerous, including Afghanistan, where he shadowed anti-Taliban forces in bullet-pocked Kabul. As the *Inquirer*'s correspondent in Africa from 1996 to 2002, Andy covered the blood feud between Ethiopia and Eritrea, genocide in Rwanda, apartheid in South Africa, and famine in Zimbabwe. But Andy was unassuming, not full of himself. I watched him flip through search warrants and wondered if he viewed the self-inflicted bloodlust between *Inquirer* and *Daily News* staff as absurd.

There was Joseph Slobodzian, or Joe Slo, an *Inquirer* reporter since 1982, who'd covered federal courts in Philadelphia for almost two decades.

On yet another day, we walked into the room to find Gail Shister, the *Inky*'s prickly former TV columnist. Gail had written about television for a quarter of a century, or, as she put it, since "God was a boy." She wasn't just a columnist; she was an *Inky* brand with her own link on the Drudge Report, a news website that got 2 million hits a day. Gail prided herself on unearthing celebrity dirt and knowing which TV shows were cued up for the morgue before the actors themselves. When CBS wanted to dump Katie Couric from the *Evening News*, Gail broke the story. On Gail's Facebook page, she posted a favorite quote (from Alice Roosevelt Longworth, the saucy daughter of Theodore Roosevelt): "If you haven't got anything good to say about anybody, come sit next to me."

Gail knew she could be caustic. She recognized herself in the best-selling novel *Good in Bed*, written by *Inquirer* colleague Jennifer Weiner. Though Weiner denied it, Gail suspected that the Gabby character, a sharp-tongued newsroom gossip, was modeled after her.

In 2007, Gail fell out of favor with *Inky* editors. They killed her TV column and booted her to the Metro desk. She was bitter about the reassignment, and the last place she wanted to be was the search warrant room.

Gail's editor, Rose Ciotta, expected Gail to pull and copy all of Jeff's search warrants. During a cell-phone call, Rose instructed Gail to use her own money to cover the copying costs—25 cents a page—and the *Inquirer* would reimburse her.

"You know how much this is going to cost?" Gail said, heatedly. "I'm not using my lunch money for this." She looked at us, all pissy, and threw open a hand in a gesture that conveyed, "Can you believe this bitch?"

Barbara and I smiled, simpatico, and Gail hung up with Rose. "Even if I had a million dollars in cash, I'm not going to use my own money," she spat. Gail was fifty-six and openly gay. She paired her foul mouth with a truck-stop wardrobe of oversize jeans and flannel shirts and sported a short and choppy hairdo that looked like she cut it herself.

Rose was a control freak with corkscrew curls that she dyed black using "a hair color called Snow Tire," an *Inky* reporter joked. Rose relentlessly rode reporters, but on this battle, she wasn't going to win. So she sent another reporter, cash in hand, to meet Gail at the courthouse. Gail and Rose were like two stag beetles, horns locked, each battling to flip the other over onto her back. They shared Buffalo roots and an upstate New York twang, but little else. When Jeff Greenfield, a senior political correspondent with CBS News, came to the *Inky* newsroom to interview Gail for a story, Gail introduced Rose: "This is Rose. Before she worked here, she was a guard at Auschwitz."

Barbara and I didn't know which was funnier—the fact that Gail was bickering with Rose over the search warrants, or that the *Inquirer* was scrounging up change to make copies, while Barbara and I had cooked up a system to Xerox for free.

On this day, we were twitchy. We couldn't let *Inky* reporters figure out that we had moved past Jeff and Benny and were now focused on bodegas raided by any cop in Jeff's squad. We pulled out a stack of search warrants, flipped through the pages, and set aside the ones we wanted to copy—facedown. Once they'd been copied, we reshuffled them like blackjack dealers into the stack.

We tried to hide our joy when we picked up a folder that *Inky* reporters had just scoured to find warrants they'd copied, lumped together, on top of a neat pile. They were all warrants we'd pulled weeks ago.

Back in the newsroom, Barbara and I spread out the search warrants on a conference table. We were amazed by how many stores Jeff and his squad had raided over a two-year period. Sometimes they hit two stores in one afternoon.

In six months alone, Jeff's squad and another squad, which included Jeff's brother, Richard, raided twenty-two bodegas, boutiques, tobacco shops, and other stores for drug paraphernalia. That number was seven times more than the unit's ten other squads combined. Those ten squads—made up of more than a hundred officers—had raided only three stores during the same period.

One of my best sources was a cop assigned to one of those ten other squads. I had met the cop, who we'll call Ray, in 2007 when I first joined the *Daily News* and was covering a story about a perv lawyer who got caught naked in a courthouse conference room with a fourteen-year-old girl. My job was to get reaction from people in the courthouse. I was outside a courtroom when I spotted Ray, his back resting against the wall as if he were seated on a comfy recliner instead of a stone bench. I walked by slowly, staring at him as I mulled over whether to approach him about the perv lawyer.

"Hey, how ya doing?" he asked.

Ray had a bright smile and a warm, casual way about him. He wore blue jeans and a neatly pressed pin-striped dress shirt. Turned out, Ray was an undercover narcotics cop like Jeff.

Yeah, he knew the perv lawyer or knew of him, but couldn't be quoted. The police department had strict rules about giving information or quotes to the news media. Ray could get in big trouble for talking to me.

I gave Ray my card, and he began to call me with story tips, like a big drug bust done by his squad or a cop who got caught with a racially offensive sticker in his locker. The sticker was a cartoon of a man, half as an officer in uniform and half as a Klansman, with the words BLUE BY DAY—WHITE BY NIGHT.

Ray was ballsy and almost cavalier about feeding me information. He'd meet me on a street corner near my office and slip me internal police documents. He'd make jokes about the clandestine handoff. "I should be wearing a trench coat and a fedora hat," he'd say.

We instantly hit it off, and he became not only a great source but a good friend. He sometimes called me just to talk, like when his ex-wife was acting nutty or his kid was doing poorly in school. He had an offbeat sense of humor and a reputation among other cops as a jokester who never let the job of chasing down drug dealers and dopers get to him. When I saw him in the courthouse, I pretended not to know him. He was often at the center of a cluster of cops, all laughing and talking and slapping each other's backs. Everyone seemed to like him.

I could rely on Ray to tell it to me straight. He believed that right was right and wrong was wrong. Even if he was the one doing the wrong, he'd own up to it. During the Tainted Justice series, I called him a lot to take his temperature, to get his perspective as a drug cop who managed informants. He once met me at a library and patiently detailed the anatomy of a drug bust, from the initial drug buy to the search-warrant application and the dos and don'ts of house raids. One day I asked Ray if female cops thought Jeff was good-looking.

"I think a lot of cops think Jeff has sugar in his tank," he said.

"What? Sugar in his tank? What does that mean?" I asked, laughing.

"Gay," he said, with his trademark bluntness.

When I called Ray to ask what he thought about all the store raids, I wasn't surprised to learn that he had only done a handful of baggie busts in his twelve years as a narcotics cop.

Jeff and Ray, though in different squads, were both part of the narcotics field unit. The elite unit was supposed to go after big fish—kingpins who headed violent drug organizations that packaged and distributed mounds of poison, bringing entire neighborhoods to their knees. Arresting shop owners on misdemeanor charges for selling tiny ziplock bags was like shooting fish in a barrel. Store-raid jobs were the smallest of small-time.

Barbara and I divvied up the search warrants. We knew there was something there, but we didn't want to prompt store owners. We decided to avoid leading questions like "Did the police dismantle your surveillance cameras?" or "Did the officers take any merchandise or money?"

"Agreed," Barbara said, and we went to work.

"Hi, I'm not sure I have the right number. I'm looking for the owner of Dominguez Grocery Store?" I heard Barbara say into her phone.

I got on the phone with another shop owner. "I'm a reporter with the *Daily News*, and I wanted to ask you about the police raid on your store," I said.

My eyes widened as I took notes. When I got off the phone, I jumped up and ran toward Barbara, who was already halfway to my desk.

"Wendy! You're never going to believe this!" she shouted.

"I know! I know," I said.

Officer Jeffrey Cujdik, of the Philadelphia Police Department's Narcotics Field Unit. He recruited Benny Martinez as Confidential Informant 103. *(David Maialetti/Staff Photographer/*Philadelphia Daily News*)*

Raul Nieves's lawyer Stephen Patrizio was the first person to suspect something was amiss. *(Yong Kim/Staff Photographer/*Philadelphia Daily News*)*

The row house at 1939 East Pacific Street that Jeff Cujdik rented to Benny Martinez, below market rate, as part of their arrangement. *(Courtesy of the authors)*

Michael Days, editor of the *Philadelphia Daily News*. *(Jessica Griffin/Staff Photographer/*Philadelphia Daily News*)*

RY BREAD:
$54M, 3 YEARS
PHILLIES, PAGES 94-92

GRAMMYS: MUSIC,
GLITTER, DRAMA
CHRIS BROWN ASSAULT PROBE: PAGE 12

PHILADELPHIA
DAILY
NEWS
THE PEOPLE PAPER

A COP AND AN INFORMANT
GOT TOO CLOSE AND
BENT THE RULES.
NOW, THE INFORMANT
FEARS FOR HIS LIFE.

TAINTED JUSTICE?

PAGE 3

The first article about Benny Martinez, featuring a silhouette photograph of him to conceal his identity, ran on the front page of the February 9, 2009, edition of the *Philadelphia Daily News* under a headline that would come to define the series. *(Courtesy of Philadelphia Daily News)*

Lady Gonzalez, the first woman to say that she was sexually assaulted by a Philadelphia Narcotics Field Unit officer during a raid. *(Sarah J. Glover/Staff Photographer/Philadelphia Daily News)*

Brian Tierney *(right)*, owner of the *Philadelphia Daily News*, after the first day of the 2009 bankruptcy hearing at Philadelphia's Federal Courthouse. *(Elizabeth Robertson/Staff Photographer/ Philadelphia Inquirer)*

From left: Philadelphia police commissioner Charles Ramsey; Janice Fedarcyk, special agent in charge of the FBI's Philadelphia field office; and Mayor Michael Nutter at a joint press conference held on February 13, 2009, to address Wendy and Barbara's story. *(Alejandro A. Alvarez/Staff Photographer/Philadelphia Daily News)*

John McNesby, president of the Philadelphia Fraternal Order of Police, speaks out against the *Philadelphia Daily News* at a February 25, 2009, press conference. George Bochetto, Jeff Cujdik's lawyer, is on the right. *(David Maialetti/Staff Photographer/Philadelphia Daily News)*

Just some of the boxes of search warrants that Wendy and Barbara waded through for their stories. *(Courtesy of the authors)*

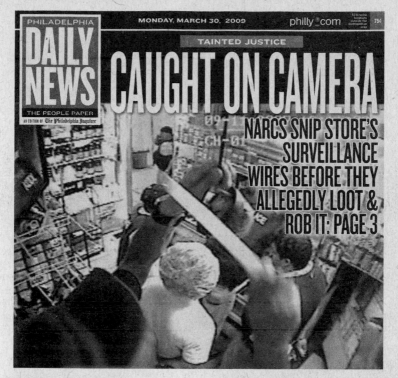

PHILADELPHIA

DAILY NEWS

THE PEOPLE PAPER
AN EDITION OF The Philadelphia Inquirer

MONDAY, MARCH 30, 2009   philly●com   75¢

TAINTED JUSTICE

CAUGHT ON CAMERA

NARCS SNIP STORE'S SURVEILLANCE WIRES BEFORE THEY ALLEGEDLY LOOT & ROB IT: PAGE 3

This frame of surveillance video from Jose Duran's store shows Narcotics Field Unit officer Anthony Parrotti polsed to cut the camera wires with a bread knife. The frame was run on the front page of the March 30, 2009, edition of the *Philadelphia Daily News. (Courtesy of Jose Duran and Philadelphia Daily News)*

Another still, which was published in the *Philadelphia Daily News* with faces blurred, shows Narcotics Field Unit officer Thomas Tolstoy *(foreground)* checking out the camera. Cujdik is directly behind him. Tolstoy was identified by at least three women as the officer who sexually assaulted them during raids. *(Courtesy of Jose Duran)*

The aftermath of the Philadelphia Narcotics Unit raid on Jose Duran's store. *(Courtesy of Jose Duran)*

Angel Castro hugs his Thayer Street neighbor Dagma Rodriguez, another woman who said she was assaulted by Officer Tolstoy. *(David Maialetti/Staff Photographer/*Philadelphia Daily News*)*

TAINTED JUSTICE

AFTER SHE REPORTED A DRUG COP'S INDECENT ASSAULT — SO ROUGH IT SENT HER TO THE HOSPITAL — THE TERRIFYING, ANONYMOUS PHONE CALLS BEGAN

'NAOMI' IN FEAR

PAGE 3

"Naomi," the third of Officer Tolstoy's alleged sexual assault victims to come forward, appears in silhouette on the cover of the June 17, 2009, edition of the *Philadelphia Daily News*. *(David Maialetti/Staff Photographer/*Philadelphia Daily News, *courtesy of* Philadelphia Daily News*)*

The photograph of Wendy with her father that Wendy slipped under her pillow for luck the night before the 2010 Pulitzer Prize announcements. *(Courtesy of Wendy Ruderman)*

Before the Pulitzer announcement, Barbara drew strength by praying to her mother. This photo of Barbara's mother sat on her desk. *(Courtesy of Barbara Laker)*

City editor Gar Joseph, Barbara *(center)*, and Wendy react to the news of their Pulitzer Prize win on April 12, 2010. *(Sarah J. Glover/Staff Photographer/*Philadelphia Daily News*)*

Brian Tierney, about to throw the ceremonial first pitch at a Phillies game, wears a shirt that captures the spirit of the *Philadelphia Daily News. (Yong Kim/Staff Photographer/*Philadelphia Daily News*)*

17

PHILADELPHIA WAS HOME TO ONE OF THE LARGEST AND FASTEST-GROWING IMMIGRANT POPULATIONS IN THE NORTHEAST, PARTLY BECAUSE THE cost of living was lower than in other cities like New York. Between 2000 and 2006, 113,000 immigrants flocked to Philly, nearly as many as had arrived in the entire decade of the 1990s. The majority came from Asia, Latin America, and the Caribbean. Some came to reunite with relatives or work at the city's numerous hospitals, tech firms, or universities. Others were entrepreneurs who opened shops with the belief that if they worked long and hard enough, they'd earn a decent living.

Bodegas could be found on almost every other block in all four corners of the city. Immigrants ran them and patronized them. At these shops, both the food and the language were familiar. Without nearby supermarkets or cars, the people in these neighborhoods bought everything there.

Barbara and I had split up the search warrants, and we began to track down the merchants. Most spoke little to no English. I'd taken five years of Spanish in high school and college; Barbara had studied French just as long. But all we remembered were textbook-taught phrases like "Excuse me, sir, can you direct me to the toilet?" or "Do you know what time the train arrives from Madrid?"

None of that would help when we talked to store owners from the Dominican Republic or Haiti. Or Korea. So we overcame the language barrier by using their relatives, store clerks, and customers to translate. Sometimes we resorted to hand signs and gestures, almost like a humorless game of charades.

When Barbara walked into a cigar and tobacco shop, she was struck by the brittle and slight appearance of the owners. Almost birdlike, the Korean couple, Du Hyon "David" and Yun Lois "Eunice" Nam, stood behind a long pane of bulletproof glass. Eunice handed lottery tickets to a customer through an opening in the protective divide, just large enough for a hand.

The Nams earned a middle-class life the hard way. They didn't expect handouts and paid their taxes. They toiled away at their store ten hours a day, six days a week, and commuted two hours a day to and from their store. David had left Seoul for the Philadelphia area in 1981 with a master's degree in foreign trade. He first opened a deli, then the smoke shop. "America Dream," he told Barbara with a bashful smile.

Barbara empathized with the Nams. Barbara was born on a chicken farm in Kent, England, about fifty miles south of London. She came to the United States with her parents and younger brother by way of the storm-tossed Atlantic in the bowels of Cunard's *QE2*. She arrived as a homesick, gangly twelve-year-old with a thick British accent. They moved to the Chicago suburbs, where kids teased her, threw paint at her front door, and beat up her younger brother—once with fists, another time with a bag of dry cement that they smashed over his head. "Why can't you leave us alone? We're not hurting you," Barbara yelled.

As a teen, Barbara wanted so desperately to fit in that she used money, earned through chores and babysitting, to buy audiotapes of people speaking with American accents. Every night after homework, Barbara listened to the tapes and parroted the words until she'd purged her British accent.

Every once in a while, I'd catch Barbara using an English expression. When she didn't quite catch what someone was telling her, she'd politely say, "Pardon?" I was more inclined to say, in my brassy toot, "Huh? Hold on. Back up. What the hell are ya talkin' about?"

In broken English, the Nams recounted the sweltering July afternoon in 2007 when Jeff and four squad members raided their shop.

"I so scared," Eunice told Barbara.

Eunice was fifty-six years old, just under five-two, and didn't weigh more than a hundred pounds. She had a tiny sliver of a nose and smooth skin, with a few faint lines around her deep-set eyes and thin lips. She didn't wear a smidge of makeup. With short, thin, curly black hair and brown-framed eyeglasses, she favored loose-fitting black pants, simple, nondescript T-shirts, and sensible flats. She was all business, just like her sixty-two-year-old husband, who was only five-seven, had a receding hairline, and hiked his pants high above his waist with a thin black belt, making his 120-pound frame appear even smaller.

Jeff and his squad blazed into the shop, screaming words

the Nams didn't understand. The cops weren't wearing their dress blues, and the terrified couple thought they were being robbed.

"They put us on floor," Eunice told Barbara, pointing to the square vinyl tiles. "Handcuffs on me," she said, clasping her spindly fingers behind her back.

"They had guns. Gun on my head," she said. "Me on floor. Stand over with gun." Eunice curled her three fingers into her palm and used her index finger and thumb to form the shape of a gun.

"Then I, how do you say?" she said as she swept her right hand toward her crotch and moved it down her thigh. "I all wet."

Barbara looked to David, who spoke a bit more English. "She wet her pants?" Barbara asked.

"Yes. Yes!" he answered, nodding his head up and down frantically, his dark eyes widening.

"I so, so scared, I wet my pants," Eunice said, shaking her head in embarrassment.

The cops smashed their two surveillance cameras with a metal rod and yanked camera wires from the ceiling. David, who stood in front of a small radio playing Korean music, showed Barbara; he pulled his hands back as if he held a golf club and then took hard, ferocious swings into the air, toward his new surveillance camera.

"Over and over, they hit. They broke it," David said.

The officers rifled through drawers, dumped dozens of cigarette cartons on the floor, and swiped cash from the registers. Then they hauled the Nams to jail for selling the baggies. When David and Eunice later unlocked the store, they discovered that a case of lighter fluid and handfuls of Zippo lighters were missing. Cops wrote in paperwork that they seized $2,573 in the raid, but the Nams said they actually had between $3,800 and $4,000 in the store. Most of their cash came in lottery sales to customers who hoped they were one lucky number away from a Powerball jackpot in the millions.

No matter the language—Korean, Arabic, Spanish, Cantonese—the merchants' stories translated the same: the cops barreled into the stores, guns drawn, spewing curse words and slurs like *mama-san*, a derogatory term typically used for a woman who runs a brothel. They sometimes shoved or struck the merchants, tying their hands behind their backs in plasticuffs— plastic handcuffs that bit into their skin. They smashed video surveillance cameras with sledgehammers or metal rods, or cut camera wires with knives they took from the store deli.

When the cameras went dark, the cops stole thousands of dollars in cash and pillaged the stores, guzzling energy drinks and scarfing down Cheez-Its and Little Debbie fudge brownies. They inhaled bags of sunflower seeds, spitting the salty shells on the floor, and helped themselves to fresh turkey hoagies, not bothering to close the refrigerated deli case, leaving the meat and cheese to spoil. They left deep fryers filled with hot vegetable oil simmering on high, not caring if the store burned to the ground. Hopped up on power, the cops swiped the shelves bare, carting off brown boxes filled with cigarettes, batteries, and canned goods. A Hispanic woman who worked at a Dominican-owned store put it simply: "It was like they was shopping."

The merchants were financially ruined—robbed with a badge—but somehow they were the criminals. The cops arrested them on either misdemeanor charges or felony charges that the court then knocked down to misdemeanors. Immigrants with no criminal records—all living here legally—found themselves being dragged through Philly's archaic justice system. They shelled out thousands of dollars in bail and attorneys' fees. They lost thousands more because their stores were shuttered for days or weeks after the raids. Some were so shaken that they closed their stores for good. Their cases took months to weave through an overburdened criminal court, costing taxpayers money. In the end, a judge sentenced them to probation and fines or lesser penalties.

The drug paraphernalia laws in Pennsylvania were open to dubious interpretation. It was only a crime to sell the baggies if the merchant knew, or should have known, that the buyer intended to use them to package drugs. The merchant had to figure out whether the customer wanted to use the bags for drugs or for some legitimate reason, like preserving rare coins or jewelry. Cops were supposed to target stores, like tire or electronics shops, which would have no reason to sell baggies. Jeff's squad should have never raided merchants like the Nams and Samir, because they had smoke shops and they sold baggies to customers who bought loose tobacco.

To make their case, cops or informants had to walk into the store and specifically ask for "weed bags" or "rock bags." That's assuming merchants, particularly those who struggled with English, were schooled in drug lingo.

Granted, most baggie buyers weren't little old ladies who wanted to store sweater buttons, earrings, or high-blood-pressure medication. They were corner drug dealers who used the baggies to peddle street-size quantities of drugs. Tiny empty baggies were discarded everywhere—playgrounds, empty lots, alleys, sidewalks. Baggies were the conduit of the drug trade. "It's like selling bullets and saying, 'We're not selling the guns, we're only selling the bullets,' " a police detective explained to Barbara and me. Some shop owners disagreed: "It's the equivalent of getting locked up for selling knives, and police saying it's murder paraphernalia," countered one merchant.

Most store owners knew that the baggies were being used to package drugs. But this was Philly. It wasn't the kind of town where you chirpily asked, "What exactly do you need those little bags for?" That could get your head blown off.

These weren't the mom-and-pop stores of yesteryear, when merchants knew their customers by name and didn't worry if they were short on cash or left their wallets at home. Back then, they'd say, "No problem, we'll settle up next time."

Many merchants bought or rented corner stores in drug-sick neighborhoods devoid of big-chain supermarkets, and of law and order. They were often afraid of their clientele, barricading themselves behind thick, scratched-up walls of bulletproof plastic and exchanging money and goods through a small slit. At least once or twice a year, a merchant got gunned down during a robbery. They invested in video-surveillance systems with multiple cameras pointed at every corner of the store. It wasn't unusual for police to show the store's grainy footage at news conferences when asking the public for help identifying armed perps.

The stores were vulnerable to robberies because the merchants typically dealt in all cash. In one day, they'd take in thousands of dollars in lottery, cigarette, and phone card sales. They used cash to pay wholesale grocery vendors and store rent or mortgages.

Jenny Lu, a fifty-one-year-old Chinese immigrant who arrived here via Vietnam, where she and her husband were fishermen, was a prisoner in her own store. Though she owned a home in South Philadelphia, she rarely slept there. Most nights, she'd lock up the shop and head upstairs to a small apartment with a bed. Jenny's store had been burglarized six times. Break-ins usually happened when the building was empty. Jenny sat sentry over her store—and her money, which she stashed under the bed mattress—like a little hamster, Jenny's daughter, Anh, liked to say.

For Jenny, it seemed safer to keep the money hidden above her store. Walking to the bank with wads of cash in her purse was dangerous. When Jeff, his brother Richard, and three other cops raided Jenny's store, she had more than $10,000, mostly in small bills, stuffed in a plastic bag under the bed. The cops upended the mattress and took it all.

Jenny, like all the other merchants we'd found, never reported the theft to police. Why would they? They came from countries where cops were notoriously corrupt. "Back home, police get away with everything, including murder," explained Danilo Burgos, president of the city's Dominican Grocers Association. Besides, what if criminals without badges robbed their stores, and they called 911? They couldn't risk being blacklisted by district cops.

18

AT FIRST THE MERCHANTS WERE RE-
LUCTANT TO TRUST BARBARA AND
ME. THEY DIDN'T WANT THEIR NAMES,
STORE LOCATIONS, OR FACES PRINTED
in the newspaper. They were scared of retaliation. They were willing to eat the loss,
chalking up the cop robberies as a Philly
street tax.

But little by little, as the merchants realized they weren't alone, the tide shifted.
Every time Barbara got another merchant
on board, she euphorically zipped through
the newsroom looking for me, even hunting me down in the bathroom. She looked
under each stall until she spotted my kid-
size sneakers.

"Wendy, I just got another one!" Barbara
whooped.

We'd have entire strategy meetings in
the bathroom with Barbara yelling ideas at
me over the stall door.

I decided to try to circle around to Samir,

the Jordanian smoke shop owner who was a no-show at his lawyer's office. I knew his name and the location of his store, and I thought maybe I could persuade him to add his voice to our story.

I found Samir's son, Moe, at the store, and he agreed to meet me with his dad at his house later that day. Just from a brief conversation with Moe, I could tell the father and son were close and Moe was protective of his father.

That night Samir greeted me at the door, where I slipped off my sneakers before entering the living room. As soon as I sat down, his wife served me homemade Middle Eastern sweets and hot mint tea. Moe translated.

"We have other store owners who told us the same story," I said. "They are going to go on the record and let us use their names in the paper."

Samir and his wife looked at each other and nodded. Moe would speak on behalf of the family.

Though Samir had lived in America for about seven years, he struggled with English. Samir was a massive man, at least six feet tall, with a hulking frame, big droopy eyes, black as olives, and long ears on either side of a meaty bald head. He was taciturn and shy and kept within the half-mile between his tobacco and cigar shop and his South Philadelphia row house, where he and his family spoke mostly Arabic. He politely nodded and smiled at neighbors and customers, who by all accounts saw him as a gentle giant.

Samir spent all day and most of the night ringing up lottery and cigarette sales, crammed in the narrow aisle between the counter cash register and a wall of white shelves, lined with sea-green cartons of Newports and mahogany boxes of Mavericks. He sold loose tobacco, coffee, and trail mix. He also sold tiny ziplock bags—$5 for 100.

Two years ago, on a late December afternoon, Samir had just finished tallying about $14,000 in cash from the day's sales when Jeff and six other cops burst into the store. Samir's son, Moe, arrived a few minutes later. Samir had been waiting for his twenty-one-year-old son, who manned the register while Samir walked the half-block to the bank to deposit the money.

"What's going on?" Moe asked, as a cop blocked him from going inside.

"We'll tell ya later," the cop said gruffly.

Moe panicked when he looked through the store window and saw his dad in handcuffs.

"I would like to know why you guys are locking up my dad for no reason," he said. "I'm his son."

A cop shoved Moe away from the window, and another plainclothes cop came over and said, "We're arresting your dad because he's selling drug supplies."

"What kind of drug supplies are you talking about?"

"Little baggies," the cop said.

"Those baggies that we got, we got those bags from the cigarette wholesaler, they sell them. People came in and asked for them and we got them, we started selling them," Moe said, the words pouring out.

The cops tore apart the store, while Moe watched through the window. He grew angry and suspicious when he saw one narcotics cop with a pair of pliers in his hand. The cop reached up to a surveillance camera mounted high on the wall and clipped the wires. The cop, who wore a navy blue jacket and a baseball cap, was careful to keep his head down as he cut the wires; he didn't want the camera lens to capture his face. One by one, he sliced the wires to all four security cameras.

Samir had never been arrested before, and he sat in the jail cell, feeling like a scared child.

When Moe opened the shop a few days later, he couldn't see the floor because of the mounds of dumped coffee grinds, candy wrappers, and crushed cigarette cartons. Nearly 40 cartons of Newports were missing. A cigar box, which contained about $900 from the day's lottery ticket sales, was bare, tossed to the floor. The cash register drawer sat ajar and empty, except for a few quarters, pennies, and dimes. Fourteen thousand dollars. Gone.

Jeff left a property receipt on the store counter. Moe looked at the receipt and wanted to pound the wall with his fist: $7,888. That was the amount Jeff claimed police had seized in the raid.

Samir shook his head and looked at Moe with those dark, soulful eyes. In Arabic, Samir said, "There is no way, because I know how much money I had that day. I counted it all up so I could take it to the bank and pay the wholesaler."

Samir lost more than money in the raid. He lost his dignity. Moe, who moved to the United States from Jordan a decade earlier, had to give up his job as a satellite-dish technician to take over his dad's store. After the raid, Samir was too scared to be in the store. Moe was twenty-three, with thick black hair, slightly gelled back. He had dark eyes and long lashes and a swagger and confidence not inherited from his dad.

"If he sees cops now, he freaks out," Moe said. "My dad never been in jail. My dad never been in trouble. Now he's like a little kid that got bit by a dog. He won't go out."

Ultimately, all the merchants decided to break their silence. Telling us what happened was their way of taking back control, of feeling empowered.

19

WHEN BARBARA AND I SAT DOWN TO
WRITE THE LATEST TAINTED JUSTICE
INSTALLMENT, WE HAD SEVEN STORE
OWNERS AND AN ATTORNEY REPRESENT-
ing an eighth—all on the record. Some even
agreed to be photographed. The number
of victimized merchants would more than
double in the next few weeks.

There was a collective catharsis among
merchants across the city. They were angry
and disillusioned. Once they started talking,
they didn't want to stop.

Emilio Vargas was a teenager when he
arrived in the US from the Dominican Republic. Now, at twenty-nine, he was jaded.
Emilio was so rattled by the police raid that
he walked away from his store. "I believed
in the American dream. I still do. I believed
that if you work hard, you get ahead. But everything changed after this. . . . I used to believe in justice in America. I don't know now.
It makes me question the justice system."

The story seemed to write itself—a rarity for us. We always wrote at my desk, sitting so close that the wheels of our swivel chairs sometimes clanked together and our shoulders touched. When staffers saw us hunkered down, typing with an intense, coffee-infused hysteria, they'd remark, "Oh boy, the Girls are up to something. Can't wait to read it."

Barbara and I sometimes struggled in our writing. On those stories, we used all kinds of excuses to procrastinate. I'd get a cup of tea. Barbara checked in with her kids at college. We ran upstairs to get trail mix from the cafeteria and chatted up other reporters during bathroom breaks.

Not with this story. The words came fast, and I only stopped typing long enough to high-five Barbara. "I love it! Do you love it?"

"Yeah, I love it," Barbara said.

We were amped up. What the cops had done to these store owners was an outrage, and we couldn't understand how the cops got away with stealing from these merchants for so long. The looting went on for years at stores all across the city, and no one said a word. It was a story hiding in plain sight, and these merchants were easy pickings.

The raid on Jenny Lu's store left her saddled with debt. The cops took every nickel, between $10,000 and $12,000, which Jenny needed to pay two mortgages, one on the store, the other on her house. She owed money to soda and food vendors and utility companies. Jenny, whose husband had died of lung cancer, was forced to close the store and take a cashier's job at a Chinatown supermarket, where she worked twelve hours a day, six days a week, earning $1,200 to $1,400 a month.

The thing, Jenny and her adult children, who helped run the store, had followed the rules. Jenny's twenty-five-year-old daughter, Anh, didn't take shit from anyone. When customers came in and asked for baggies, she'd question, point-blank, "What do you need them for?" If they muttered "Weed" or "Crack," she'd always say, "I'm sorry, we don't have any of those bags."

Prosecutors initially charged Jenny, who was barely over five feet tall and 110 pounds, with a felony because of the large number of baggies found in her store. The city district attorney's office moved to seize the store through drug forfeiture. Jenny called Anh collect from the jail at 3:00 a.m. and told her to post bail. "Are you serious?" Anh asked when she got to the police station. "A fifty-one-year-old lady in clogs committing a felony?"

Barbara and I were close to finishing the story about the merchants when we contacted Jeff's attorney, George Bochetto. We already knew that there was no reason for cops to smash the stores' video surveillance systems and yank the wires from the ceiling. I had passed it by Ray, and Barbara had done the same with a high-ranking police source. Both cops told us that destroying cameras wasn't part of any police protocol and was actually in violation of a directive that read, "Unnecessary damage or destruction of personal property by police during a search is strictly prohibited and WILL result in severe disciplinary action." We couldn't imagine how George was going to defend Jeff on this one.

George's response was quintessential George. "Now that the *Daily News* has created a mass hysteria concerning the Philadelphia Narcotics Unit, it comes as no surprise that every defendant ever arrested will now proclaim their innocence and bark about being mistreated," he e-mailed.

We filed the story to Gar and watched him disappear into his office to read it. He seemed gone for a long while. Then at 6:40 p.m., right around the time Barbara and I wondered whether we should grab dinner, an e-mail popped up on my computer. It was from Gar, with a single subject line: "This might be the best story I've edited in my entire career."

Barbara and I were stunned. Gar was the Ebenezer Scrooge of the compliment department. His e-mail was totally out of character, akin to planting sloppy wet kisses on our cheeks.

Gar's office was no bigger than a handicapped-bathroom stall and kind of smelled like one. Glue mouse traps, sprinkled with bait pellets, sat under his computer and behind the door. Mice had burrowed into the cushions of a small, faded black couch pushed against the wall. We sat down and caught a whiff of death. We suspected that at least one mouse was dead somewhere, a sofa coil wrapped around its tiny neck.

On the wall directly above Gar's computer, next to the "Despair" poster, was a reprint of a locomotive train emerging from the ornate and Gothic former Broad Street Station on the Pennsylvania Railroad. Gar, whose grandfather had worked as a railroad machinist, was one of those quirky adults who still loved trains. No one—and nothing—could beat the boy out of Gar, not even years of editing incomprehensible stories written by reporters with borderline personalities.

Gar had a love-hate relationship with his job. "It's very manic-depressive. I'm either so fuckin' depressed that I want to quit or I feel on top of the world because we've got a great story."

He was having an on-top-of-the-world kind of day.

"We got these sons of bitches, dead to rights! We got 'em. We got 'em!" Gar screeched gleefully after finishing the edit.

Gar wanted reporters to see him as a gruff and hardened editor. But he secretly teared up when he read a poignant story, one with heart. "This is not fuckin' brain surgery," he said about journalism. "It's simple. Write stories that evoke emotion, that make readers cry or laugh or get outraged or disgusted, and give them their money's worth."

That night, Gar went home and told his wife, Marty, "We have a great story coming out tomorrow." Marty knew not to ask for any details, including the general topic. As a longtime *Inquirer* reporter who covered the education beat, Marty was, technically, the enemy. Marty was the reporter who showed up at the search warrant room to give Gail money for copies. Of all the *Inky* reporters at Rose's whim, she chose to dispatch the wife of our editor. In all of their twenty-four years of marriage, Gar and Marty worked at Philly's rival papers. Staying married meant no shop talk.

Barbara got home around midnight. She was greeted by her dog, Seven, a name Barbara's daughter got from a *Seinfeld* episode in which George says he would name his firstborn child Seven after Mickey Mantle's jersey number. Seven was a rescue mutt with a pointy face and a mop of long, wavy brown, gold, and white hair over a Corgi-like sausage body. Barbara always felt guilty when she worked this late. Seven was crazed for attention and followed Barbara all around the house, her bushy tail sweeping the worn oak. With her three-inch legs, Seven had to angle her body to get down the steps.

Barbara ate like a single woman on a budget. She opened a can of fat-free vegetarian baked beans and grabbed a box of wheat crackers from a kitchen cabinet. As the beans heated in the microwave, she poured a glass of $8.99-a-bottle chardonnay and sat on the couch to watch *Nightline*. She capped off dinner with a Tylenol PM and went to bed.

I came home to find Karl, pajama-clad in plaid flannel, seated in his leather maroon recliner, rubbing Icy Hot into the arches of his bare feet. Karl, who jogged every other

morning, liked to say that Icy Hot was the cologne of choice
for middle-aged men who exercised. Karl was in front of
the TV, watching one of his home-improvement shows. The
entire living room reeked of menthol. He was in the throes of
his make-your-own-furniture phase, having recently cobbled
together a pair of faux-leather chairs. The cushions hung so
far past the wooden frame that brave friends who sat down
unexpectedly slid to the floor.

This was around the time that Karl started calling our
Tainted Justice series "T'ain't Been Home in Weeks." As
usual, Karl left my dinner in the fridge on a plate covered
with Saran Wrap. And as usual, it was his usual: penne pasta
sautéed in olive oil, fresh spinach, and garlic. I took two bites
and buried the rest in the trash can.

The next morning, I ran out my front door to get the
newspaper. My stomach fluttered with excitement. There was
nothing like seeing your story on the front page, especially
one this powerful and explosive. The headline trumpeted,
"Smash & Grab: Shopkeepers say narcotics cops disabled security cameras, looted and trashed their stores." Underneath
the headline was a photo of a bodega owner. He stood in
front of his store with his arms crossed and a defiant scowl on
his face. Bam.

The *Inquirer* had nothing. Yeah, we really got "mercilessly
pounded" on that one, I thought.

20

THE FBI AGENTS ON THE POLICE-
CORRUPTION CASE READ THE BODEGA
STORY AND FLIPPED OUT. THEY DIDN'T
KNOW ABOUT THE STORE ROBBERIES
because Benny didn't know about them. All
Benny knew was that Jeff sometimes gave
him cartons of cigarettes and other goods.
Now the FBI had to follow us. Agents imme-
diately fanned out to interview store owners.
This gave Barbara and me a little thrill, but
we doubted that the FBI was overjoyed.

We were "feeling our oats," as my mom
always said when I got all cocky and full of
my pint-size self, when my phone rang at
work.

"This Wendy? I have video. Backup," the
man on the other end said.

"What? Did you say video? Of a raid on
your store?"

"Yeah. Yeah. Video. I got computer hid.
They went crazy looking for computer," he
said. "I got copy."

"A copy? Of the video?" I said, practically yelling into my phone.

Jose Duran had come to the United States some thirteen years earlier, but his English was a nightmare. It's not that he didn't speak the language. He did. Only with an accent that smothered his words like a wet wool blanket. He had a high-pitched gravelly voice that reminded me of Tattoo, the midget who played Mr. Roarke's assistant on the TV series *Fantasy Island*. I asked Jose if I could get the tape that night. He gave me his address in New Jersey. He lived only five miles from my house.

I turned into his long driveway, and even in the dark, I could see that the house was a stately colonial with a wide front porch framed by ornate white columns. The three-story house, set back from the street, was parchment yellow with dark shutters. Oh shit, I thought, I hope he isn't some kind of big-time drug dealer.

Jose answered the door. He was stout, with a thick helmet of black hair and dark eyebrows, like two bushy caterpillars. He wore khaki pants, tan leather loafers, and a sweater with a dress shirt underneath. He had a long vertical scar on his forehead from when, as a thirteen-year-old in the Dominican Republic, he crashed a motorized dirt bike into a utility pole with a nail that ripped into his skin.

Jose was only twenty-eight, and at the time of the raid, he ran a bodega in Philly and a mini-mart in New Jersey. Turned out, Jose shared the house with a nest full of relatives, including his sister, her husband, and their kids. He handed me a copy of a CD containing ten minutes of footage, including audio. I knew from the search warrant that Jeff's squad had raided Jose's bodega, with Jeff's brother, Richard, in charge.

It was about 9:30 p.m., and I called Barbara from Jose's driveway, shrieking, "I got it. I got it!" Then I called Karl.

"I'm on my way home. I was gonna stop by the grocery store. Do you need anything?"

"Yeah, a wife," he said, and we both laughed.

I couldn't sleep that night, thinking about Jose's CD in my black vinyl work bag. When I got to work the next morning, the first thing I did was call my cop source, Ray. Barbara and I wanted him to see the tape. We knew what Jeff looked like, but we needed Ray to help identify the other cops and school us on what was police protocol—and more importantly, what wasn't. Ray was nearby at the criminal courthouse and said he'd be right over.

In the two years I'd known Ray, we'd never met in the newsroom. This was a big risk for him. What if another cop saw him going into the *Daily News* building? Ray's curiosity won out over good sense. There was nothing surreptitious about his entrance into the newsroom. He strutted down the center aisle with a toothy grin.

Barbara had put the CD in computers all over the newsroom, but couldn't get it to play on any of them. Everything at the *Daily News* was janky. The computers were bulky and sounded like jet planes taking off whenever we turned them on. Barbara, Ray, and I walked over to a graphic artist who was computer-savvy to see if he could get the tape to play. Still, no go. Damn it. Damn this washboard newspaper with its old-timey technology.

We knew we'd have to drive back to Jose's house to play the tape. To our surprise, Ray offered to go with us. Barbara checked out a company car and Ray stretched his legs out in the back of a PT Cruiser, one of about a dozen fleet cars shared by reporters at both newspapers. Barbara drove.

I told Ray that my driving scared Barbara because I was a nervous, brake-stomping wheel-jerker. I couldn't get my mind around the idea that we humans are really nothing more than souped-up monkeys who vroom down highways at eighty miles per hour, sometimes doing so while applying lipstick or texting or reading MapQuest directions. Even I was guilty of tweezing my mustache hairs while driving. I hated the idea of entrusting strangers to stay in their own lanes while driving and often thought how the only thing separating me and my car from a horrific crash, possibly death, was an imaginary barrier in the form of a white painted line. As I was explaining my driving phobia to Ray, I looked at Barbara, who gripped the steering wheel tighter and darted her head from left to right to check her side mirrors.

"You're freakin' me out," Barbara said as she changed lanes.

We arrived at Jose's house by late afternoon. Jose and Ray shook hands in the foyer. "Ray is a friend. He's helping us with the story," I offered with a shrug.

Jose was a savvy guy; he didn't ask too many questions. He led us to the dining room, where a computer sat at the head of a polished wood table with a glass chandelier overhead. Jose's wife flitted in and out of the kitchen, offering iced tea and snacks.

Jose told us he was a technology buff who loved to tinker with computers and electronic gadgets. After high school, he studied electronics at a trade school in the Bronx. He'd rigged his bodega with a sophisticated $15,000 surveillance system, which recorded video on a backup hard drive hidden behind a display of bobby pins in the store. The backup downloaded the footage to a secure Internet site that he could access from any computer.

"I record everything because sometimes I got to go out and I leave employees by themselves. That's how you find out who's doing right, who's doing wrong. Plus, the money. I got cameras watching the money," Jose explained.

The four of us huddled around Jose's computer. He slid the CD in. We instantly recognized Jose on the screen, wearing baggy knee-length jean shorts, a dark blue polo shirt, and black Adidas slider sandals with white ankle socks.

In the video, Jose paces back and forth in front of the store's ice-cream freezer, which sits in front of the cash register window. As he chats with his brother-in-law in Spanish on a cell phone, Jose's back is turned to the store's front door when the first cop bursts in. The cop, a pudgy frat-boy type, has his gun drawn. He points it at Jose's head.

Ray recognized the cop immediately. "That's Tom Tolstoy."

"The Boob Man?" Barbara asked, referring to the nickname for the cop who fondled Lady Gonzalez's breasts and was rumored to have sexually assaulted other women during raids. Barbara moved in closer to Jose's computer screen for a better look at Tolstoy's face. Tolstoy was a cross between Fred Flintstone and Bob's Big Boy, particularly with his doo-wop hairstyle. His bangs were moussed or jelled into a stiff point that swooped back, S-shaped.

"Hand me the phone! Gimme the phone," Tolstoy yells on the videotape.

"Hey, I work here," Jose says.

"Put your hands on your head!"

"I'm the owner."

"Put your hands behind your back!"

Tolstoy spins Jose around and cuffs him. Five other cops, all wearing jeans and vests or shirts emblazoned with the word POLICE, barrel into the store behind Tolstoy. At first the cops ask routine questions, presumably for their safety: Does Jose have a gun? Does anyone live on the second floor? Are there dogs in the basement?

Sergeant Joe Bologna, a beer-bellied bully with a baseball cap who supervised the raid, looks up and wags his finger toward the ceiling.

"Whaddya got, cameras over there? . . . Where are they hooked up to?" Bologna barks.

Every cop in Jose's store is fixated on the surveillance system.

"There's cameras all over the place," Jeff's brother, Richard, says. "Where's the video cameras? The cassette for it?"

"Does it record? Does it record?" Jeff quickly interjects. Standing next to Jeff, Richard appears much shorter and scrawny, lacking his brother's good looks.

Tolstoy glances up and scans the ceiling. "I got, like, seven or eight eyes."

"There's three right here," says Thomas Kuhn, a squat and chubby cop who is wearing shorts and a baseball cap on backward.

"Listen to me," Tolstoy says. "There's one outside. There is one, two, three, four in the aisles, and there's one right here somewhere."

Jose asks if he can call his wife, and Tolstoy gruffly tells him he can't call anyone. Then Tolstoy opens the cash register drawer and eyes the money, then looks up at the camera above the register, and back down at the money. His meaty frame stuffed in the narrow space behind the cash register, Tolstoy reaches up and swats at the camera lens. He can't get at it, so he walks away, comes back with a long serrated knife, and goes to work on the camera. There's a close-up of his wrist and the blade of the knife. Jeff is in the background, looking at the cash register. The camera eventually goes dark.

An outdoor camera, aimed at the street, catches Richard rummaging through Jose's white van without a search warrant.

Back inside the store, Kuhn on the other side of the counter steps up onto a blue milk crate and struggles to grab a camera above his head.

"I need to be fucking taller," Kuhn mumbles as another cop laughs.

"You got a ladder in here, cuz?" Kuhn asks Jose.

"Yo," Tolstoy calls out from behind the cash register. "Does this camera go home? Can you view this on your computer, too?"

"I can see, yeah, home, yeah," Duran replies.

"So your wife knows we're here, then?" Tolstoy asks.

"My wife? No. She not looking the computer right now."

"Hey, Sarge . . . Come 'ere," Tolstoy shouts.

Bologna waddles over to the front counter, and Jeff leans in and whispers, "There's one in the back corner right there."

Officer Anthony Parrotti, sporting a khaki military cap and a goatee, his forearms covered in tattoos, reaches up to a camera in front of the register, pulls a wire down, and slices it with a bread knife from the store's deli.

"It can be viewed at home," Tolstoy tells Bologna.

"Okay. We'll disconnect it. That's cool," Bologna assures Tolstoy.

One by one, the cops disarm and destroy all seven of Jose's cameras until the screen goes dark and the audio cuts out.

When the tape ended, we sat at Jose's table looking at each other. No one could watch that tape and not know that the cops were up to no good. We played it again, and Ray pointed out each cop by name.

"He no touch the money with the system looking at him. No, he touch the money after they destroy all the system," Jose said while watching Tolstoy behind the cash register.

"These cops are in so much fucking trouble," Ray said.

"Look at these i-d-i-o-t-s," Jose said.

"I know," Ray said, shaking his head. The two men busted out laughing, as if they were old friends.

It was a surreal scene, watching a narcotics cop and a merchant victimized by narcotics cops joking around together about the video. "He a good guy," Jose said about Ray.

After leaving Jose's, Barbara and I took Ray to Applebee's for dinner. We sat at a booth, surrounded by families with whiny toddlers in high chairs and old couples chewing their food in silence. The food was bad, the place was loud, and the service sucked. It was pure paradise. We had the goods on these cops, the video was gold—and all three of us knew it.

21

OVER THE NEXT FOUR DAYS, BARBARA
AND I WORKED LATE EACH NIGHT PUT-
TING THE STORY TOGETHER. THE MOST
LABORIOUS PART WAS TRANSCRIBING
the audio portion of the video. I spent close
to eighteen hours listening to, then pausing
and replaying, the audio. I worried that the
Daily News could get sued if I didn't get the
verbiage exact or I screwed up which cop
said what.

On one of those nights, at about 10:00
p.m., Barbara and I walked out the building's back door and got spooked when we
saw a pickup truck.

The truck was idling at the stop sign on
the narrow road that reporters crossed to
get to the parking garage. The truck had
a small flatbed and a Fraternal Order of
Police specialty license plate. Two men,
both white, glared at us from the truck's
front seat. Barbara and I froze. "Wendy,
they're cops," she said, grabbing my arm,

a gesture that grew out of Barbara's protective maternal instinct, not fear.

If they intended to hurt us, now was the time. At this hour, the area was desolate, with plenty of dimly lit crevices and alleys between closed office buildings. At least one editor had been mugged here. The corner bar, Westy's Tavern, was still open, but the place wasn't crowded on weeknights, except for Thursday karaoke nights.

The men, stone-faced, stared us down. We didn't recognize their faces from the video. Maybe they were friends of the cops on Jeff's squad. We didn't know. Barbara and I darted across the street, keeping an eye on the truck's reverse lights just in case the driver decided to flatten us. We got to our cars, parked close to one another.

"Wendy, they might follow one of us home. Make sure you lock your doors," Barbara said. "Call me as soon as you get home."

I spent the whole ride home checking my rearview window to see if the truck or some other car had followed me. Once home, I had to crawl over to the passenger door to get out because the driver's-side door, when locked, didn't open from the inside.

I checked in with Barbara; neither of us slept well that night, listening for the rumble of cars or any unusual house sounds.

By then, we'd practically memorized the store video. The cops' voices replayed in our heads. The cops unholstered their guns and stormed into Jose's store as if they were taking down Pablo Escobar or some other notorious kingpin. Not looking for a businessman selling ziplock baggies.

"You have any paraphernalia in here? Twelve-twelves," Richard says to Jose on the video.

"What you mean, twelve-twelves?" Jose asks, hands cuffed behind his back.

"The baggies. You got twelve-twelves? . . . You have some?"

"A little bit, yeah."

Jose tries to explain to Richard that he bought the store already stocked with merchandise, including baggies.

"Okay, it don't matter. You should know your business," Richard says.

Richard then inexplicably asks Jose, "You have cats in here, too?" As if he's about to get mauled by a killer tabby.

Jeff tells Jose that he has to seize the cameras as evidence. "So we gotta get rid of it. You got yourself on video selling drug paraphernalia."

"It's illegal, boss. It's illegal," Richard tells Jose.

Yeah, and it's also illegal to lie on search warrants, Barbara and I thought when we viewed the video. The fact was, Richard got captured on video selling bullshit.

In the application for the search warrant, Richard wrote that he watched as a confidential informant went into Jose's store and bought baggies at about 4:30 p.m. on a September afternoon, about two and a half hours before the store raid.

Jose's digital surveillance footage was time-stamped. Barbara and I studied the stretch of tape between 4:00 and 5:00 p.m. Not a single customer asked for or bought a ziplock bag. On top of that, the video shows Richard searching Jose's van without a warrant, which is illegal. Richard left it unlocked with the keys in the center console, so anyone could steal it.

The cops locked up Jose on misdemeanor charges, stole almost $10,000, and left his store in a shambles. Jose couldn't understand why the cops didn't just give him a warning or even a citation for having baggies in his store. "If it's illegal, okay, take it out . . . don't destroy my business and rob me," Jose said.

A judge sentenced Jose to nine months' probation.

I called Charles Ramsey, the city's police commissioner, to tell him about the video and get a comment. Ramsey couldn't think of any reason cops would destroy video surveillance cameras. "You wouldn't just cut and take it because that's somebody's private property," he said.

Ramsey wanted us to turn over the video to internal affairs and the FBI. "It's pretty serious, and I want to get to the bottom of it."

Ramsey thought that Barbara and I only cared about getting a big story. In his mind, we weren't interested in nabbing dirty cops, not really. "You're looking at something I've not seen. I've got a task force that's looking into this entire matter. They need to be informed of this and they need a chance to look at it," Ramsey said. "If we need a subpoena . . ."

"We'll give it to you. We're putting it up on our website tomorrow," I told him.

Michael Days asked me, Barbara, and Gar to come into his office.

"This video is great stuff. It's unbelievable. And when you see that cop cut those wires with the knife—wow, I mean wow," Michael said with a chortle.

Michael intended to put the entire ten-minute tape online, along with a transcript. He wanted to name names. The only question was whether we should blur the cops' faces. There wasn't any law or court opinion that forced us to do so. After all, these cops routinely testified in open court, where they faced drug dealers seated a few feet away at the defendants' table.

"You know what? I think we should take the high road on this one," Michael said. "I don't want anyone to accuse us of putting these cops' lives in danger, with them being undercover and all."

It took hours for the photo and online staff to fog the cops' faces with grayish circles and make sure the blur followed them as they moved through the bodega.

Barbara called George Bochetto, who by this point was almost crying uncle. The fight in his voice was gone. When Barbara told him about the video, he didn't ask any questions. He didn't even ask to see it.

"I stand by what I said before," he offered lamely.

Barbara and I recycled Bochetto's quote from the first bodega story in which he accused the *Daily News* of stirring up mass hysteria.

The front page was a freeze-frame of Officer Anthony Parrotti wielding a bread knife, seconds before he slices the camera wire. The headline was, "Caught on Camera: Narcs Snip Store's Surveillance Wires Before They Allegedly Loot & Rob It."

Allegedly. What a great word.

The next day, computers across the Philadelphia region kept crashing because so many people wanted to view the video. By 8:15 a.m., there were nearly a hundred reader comments posted online. That number would swell exponentially by day's end. Overwhelmingly, readers were disgusted with the cops:

Why would the *Daily News* blur the officers' faces in these shots? As members of the community, shouldn't we know what these dangerous men look like?

World's Most Stupidest Criminals.

Where's fat-neck [Fraternal Order of Police president] McNesby to defend to these scumbag heroes?

Now will someone get "Training Day" out of the Police Department Film Library? My hope is that the *Daily News* is watching out for these reporters. . . . There are too many armed thugs with badges running around masquerading as good cops.

Well, it's nice to know that the crackdown on ziplock baggies is in full swing in a city that records 300+ murders a year, and solves less than half.

Barbara and I wouldn't hear from Bochetto again.

22

AFTER SEEING THE VIDEO, COMMIS-
SIONER RAMSEY TOOK RICHARD
CUJDIK OFF THE STREET. RICHARD
JOINED HIS BROTHER AND JEFF'S PART-
ner, Robert "Bobby" McDonnell, on desk
duty, where they spent their days answering
phones and shuffling police paperwork,
their law enforcement powers virtually non-
existent. Bobby hadn't been part of the raid
on Jose's store, but he was linked to bogus
search warrants with Jeff.

Richard went around defending himself
to other cops, spinning his desk-duty stint
as a mere hiccup in his police career. He
believed he'd be back on the street soon
enough. For Richard, the months riding
a desk would stretch into years as the FBI-
led investigation crawled forward. Richard,
Jeff, and Bobby were stuck there, and Barbara and I were determined to land Officer
Thomas Tolstoy, the Boob Man, on the desk
with them.

Tolstoy's preoccupation with large-breasted women was an open secret among the cops in his squad. In fact, at least one narcotics cop from a neighboring town knew Tolstoy, a thirty-five-year-old married father of two little boys, as the Boob Man. Tolstoy was a predator, and we wanted him off the street.

Benny had told us early on that Tolstoy "fisted" a woman; at least, that's the story he heard from Jeff.

"What?" Barbara asked. She recoiled, not able to get her mind around it. "What do you mean?"

Benny blushed while explaining that Tolstoy supposedly shoved his hand up a woman's vagina during a drug raid. His words were peppered with nervous chuckles and awkward pauses.

The feds had told Benny not to talk to us. But he called constantly using throwaway Cricket Wireless phones. There were health dramas: a garage-bay door slammed down on his back at the auto dealership where he worked detailing cars. He tumbled down some steps and broke his foot. Sonia had a lump on her breast; she slipped on the sidewalk outside a doctor's office and smacked her head, which triggered a brain bleed. They made frequent trips to the hospital, mostly for painkillers, and to the offices of personal-injury lawyers.

There were Benny's I'm-gonna-die dramas: The cops were going to hire a hit man to make him "disappear." One of the drug dealers set up by Benny and Jeff got knifed in prison, and the guy's relatives wanted to retaliate against Benny. He regretted turning against Jeff and wanted to kill himself. The feds sent Benny to a therapist, but he didn't trust her.

There were money dramas: He couldn't afford the rent at his new place, and the feds weren't helping him. He didn't have money to buy his kids birthday presents. He had to sell the family's wide-screen television. He couldn't afford a defense lawyer and feared the feds might charge him with theft or fraud for accepting money for drug jobs he never did.

Behind all the drama, there was an unspoken message: Barbara and I had ruined his life by writing his story. We were to blame.

As journalists, Barbara and I couldn't give him money, but we tried to help him in other ways. We went on Apartment Finder.com to search for a cheaper place for Benny and his family to live. We called criminal defense attorneys to see if they would accept him as a client. I bought him groceries, rushing over to his home with bags of vegetables, turkey, and Dora the Explorer fruit snacks. I bought his son a Razor scooter for his birthday and told Benny to say it was from him. In retrospect, I wondered if Benny sold the scooter for drugs, but at the time, I was so plagued with guilt that I couldn't see through his manipulation and lies.

Barbara and I knew the things we did for Benny crossed the line. But that line—the one between reporter and human being—got blurry.

After we started writing about the bodegas, the FBI knew Tainted Justice was much more than a case of fabricating evidence for search warrants. It was going to get big. The FBI needed Benny to be safe, so they relocated him, Sonia, and their two kids to a fully furnished two-bedroom suite near Philadelphia International Airport. The rent was $2,600 a month, which the feds agreed to pay—at least for now. The suite, described in a brochure as a "chalet," was like no place Benny and Sonia had ever lived. It was equipped with a washer and dryer, a luxury for most people back in the hood. The decor was simple and crisp, with a taupe couch, a glass coffee table, and a dining set with high-backed chairs. Powder-blue walls offset a spotless beige carpet. The suite's front door opened up to a courtyard with a manicured lawn bordered with shrubs and flowers.

Benny watched the store-raid video on a computer in his suite. "I couldn't believe it," Benny said excitedly. "And Tolstoy . . . I was like this motherfucker, he's just a fuckin' bastard."

The Hispanic community, particularly the Dominicans, was in a furor over the bodega raids. "None of these people should have spent half a day in jail over these bullshit charges," fumed Danilo Burgos, head of the three-hundred-member Dominican Grocers Association.

One week after the *Daily News* posted Jose's video online, the city's Hispanic leaders banded together and wrote a searing letter to Ramsey. The letter, which they copied to the district attorney, a city councilwoman, and the mayor's office, called on Ramsey to crack down on bad cops.

"The fact that many reluctant businesspeople have felt compelled to come forward with their complaints, risking their livelihoods and that of their families, indicates that the problem of police abuse has reached a boiling point," Danilo and five other Hispanic leaders wrote.

Jose's video forced Ramsey to do something that his predecessors had failed to do. He took a sledgehammer to the cliquish and chummy squads within the narcotics field unit, splitting up cops who had worked side by side for years.

Seven years earlier, a police watchdog had recommended regular reshuffling of narcotics officers and their supervisors to keep cops honest and prevent abuse. Police brass had ignored the recommendation—until now.

But Ramsey's move to break up the ten narcotic squads did nothing to appease angry Hispanic leaders. "That's just shuffling the deck. It's just window dressing," one said.

Ramsey's style was to tackle thorny issues and criticism head-on. Before coming to Philadelphia in 2008, Ramsey had served as chief of police in Washington, D.C. As an outsider, Ramsey didn't care whether he was popular among Philly's rank and file. He agreed to address irate residents and merchants at a nighttime community meeting. The meeting was held at a church, not far from some of the bodegas raided by Jeff's squad.

We didn't both have to attend the meeting. One of us could have gone and written the story on deadline for the next day's paper, but neither of us wanted to miss it. Ramsey had to appease an entire community because of our stories. Typically, Barbara and I wrestled with our own insecurities, fearing that we weren't good enough or smart enough. For me, those doubts stemmed from grade school, when my teacher wanted me to repeat fourth grade and labeled me a "late bloomer," which I thought meant I was destined for the tart cart, the short blue school bus that brought "slow" kids to special ed. Barbara's doubtfulness, in part, came from her mom, an advertising sales rep who pushed herself to be No. 1, and set the bar high for Barbara. Her mom often started sentences, "The problem with you, Barbara, is . . ."

Now, at the community meeting, our insecurities were on hiatus, temporarily banished by our egos.

Ramsey stood up at the podium, looking weary, as usual. Whenever Barbara and I saw Ramsey, he looked as if he had fifty problems on his mind. The boyish freckles smattered across his face didn't seem to mesh with his trademark stoicism. Ramsey had buried slain cops and fired dirty ones, each time finding just right the words to honor or scorn.

And here, before a contentious crowd of sixty or more, Ramsey again struck just the right note. "Corruption of any kind will not be tolerated in this department, period. And those who engage in it are going to face charges both from the department as well as criminal charges."

Immediately, loud applause broke out in the church.

When the meeting ended, merchants and community leaders came over to Barbara and me. They grasped our hands in theirs and thanked us for exposing a wrong, for caring about them. I looked at Barbara and saw her green eyes moisten. We fed off their emotion and left the church feeling good about the *Daily News* and the power of journalism. At that moment, the death knell of our industry seemed remote.

23

BRIAN TIERNEY, AS CEO AND PUB-
LISHER OF THE *DAILY NEWS* AND THE
INQUIRER, WAS IN THE FIGHT OF HIS
LIFE. THE COMPANY WAS NEARLY $400
million in debt, with the economy, advertising sales, and newspaper circulation in a
tailspin.

It wasn't just Tierney's money on the
line. It was his reputation, his image. What
Tierney had once visualized as a Hollywood
script about a champion of a man who saved
a dying business was turning into a story of
doom. His dream was just that—a dream,
almost a fantasy. Tierney loved the challenge of being the underdog in a business
brawl, but this appeared insurmountable.

Tierney's group failed to reach a deal
with senior lenders, led by Citizens Bank,
to restructure the debt load. And Tierney
emerged as the protagonist in a Greek tragedy, playing out in US bankruptcy court,
that would determine the fate of Philadelphia's two largest newspapers.

He was also under fire for taking a 37 percent raise, which boosted his pay from $618,000 to $850,000 just two months before the bankruptcy filing. Leaders of the Philadelphia Newspaper Guild, the union that represented reporters, were furious because they had convinced union members to give up a $25-a-week raise to help stem the company's financial hemorrhage. Tierney, who had put $10 million of his own money into buying the papers, argued he got the raise because he was doing two jobs—CEO and publisher—which effectively saved the company $1.25 million over two years. Still, Tierney rescinded the raise amid the outcry.

Barbara and I weren't worked up over the whole Tierney raise controversy. Tierney had saved my job, and I was grateful. As long as our paychecks covered the bills and mortgages, Barbara and I were happy. We didn't wish for Friday or watch the clock, willing it to 5:00 p.m. Journalism defined us. Our identities were so entwined with our work that when we were on a good story, everything else in our lives seemed rosy. My marriage was perfect, my kids were headed for Harvard, and Barbara went on dates with a confident zing and sang Rolling Stones tunes—off-key—while driving to work.

Even while home with the kids, I was still in work mode. I talked to Barbara so often that when my cell phone rang, Brody would say, "I hope that's not Barbara wanting a playdate." Each summer Karl and I took the kids to a weekend-long YMCA family camp on a lake dotted with cabins. When I told Brody that I wanted to be in the camp talent show, he said, "What's your talent? Work? Are you going to get up there and work?"

For the first time in her journalism career, Barbara could work twelve-hour days whenever she wanted. When Josh and Anna were younger, she often had to race out at 6:00 p.m.—literally sprinting to her car—to shuttle Josh to hockey practice or Anna to dance class, and pick up the slack at home when her husband left for one of his many business trips. She had more freedom now that her kids were in college, but she felt alone. She missed the chatter and chaos of family life, and work filled a void.

As syrupy as this sounds, on most days Barbara and I saw the job as a privilege, and the Tainted Justice series affirmed it. A tidal wave was cascading over the newspaper business, with Tierney atop the peak in Philadelphia, yet Barbara and I were still on a journalism high.

Under Tierney, the *Daily News* was a favorite child. Even on Tierney's darkest days, when his boyish, contagious enthusiasm was hard to muster, he walked through the *Daily News* newsroom, a flurry of energy, wisps of hair fluttering over his ears, to catch an elevator to his executive suite. He could have avoided reporters and taken the hallway to loop around the *Daily News*, but it seemed he needed to siphon the spirit, zeal, and zaniness of the newsroom. Barbara and I thought all the chatter about stories gave Tierney a daily reminder as to why the battle was worth it.

"Love that story today about . . . ," he shouted to reporters. If not too rushed, he stopped to chat about the big story of the day.

From the jump, Tierney and the *Daily News* staff got each other. Tierney was a "bare-knuckles player in a bare-knuckles town and the *Daily News* was a bare-knuckles kind of newspaper." That's how Zack Stalberg, a *Daily News* editor for twenty years before Michael Days took the helm, summed up the relationship. Tierney also liked the fact that the *Daily News* was able to do a lot more with a lot less than the *Inquirer*. We were like a cheap date; we were low-maintenance—content to grab a Bud Light at a dive bar.

When creditors wanted to shutter the *Daily News*, not because we were bleeding money but because they thought our demise would help the *Inquirer*'s bottom line, Tierney refused. "As long as I'm running the place, the *Daily News* will never be closed."

By spring 2009, media analysts were writing print journalism's obituary. "It's the end of the newspaper business right now, this point in time," pronounced longtime media watcher Michael Wolff.

Tierney wouldn't hear it.

"We," he told CBS News, "are the originators of the investigative work that needs to be done."

24

WE SPENT HOURS IN THE OFFICE, RE-
PLAYING THE JOSE VIDEO. WE PAUSED
IT ON A CLOSE-UP OF TOLSTOY'S FACE.
WE ALREADY HAD HIS BADGE NUMBER;
now we knew what he looked like.

Of all the cops in the video, Tolstoy came
across as the biggest asshole, a caricature
of a cop on a power trip, the self-important
type who gleefully puts people in handcuffs,
making them extra tight, and slams their
heads against the cruiser to show who's boss.

We wanted Lady Gonzalez to see Jose's
video, the version without the cops' faces
blurred. The cop who sexually assaulted her
had told her to call him Tom. When Barbara and I first met Lady three months earlier, we hadn't told her the cop's full name.
We wanted to play fair; we needed Lady to
identify him without prompts from us.

Lady had grown to trust Barbara and
me, so when we asked her to come to the
office to see the raw video, she immediately

agreed. We cued up the raw video on a computer in the news-room and asked Lady to take a seat.

"Lady, we want you to look at this video and tell us if you rec-ognize the cop who fondled you. I can't tell you if he's on here, and I can't say anything while you watch it," Barbara said.

She repeatedly said she was nervous and rubbed her palms up and down the front of her blue jeans.

"Okay. I'm ready," Lady said softly before taking a deep heave of air.. Barbara pulled up a chair and sat next to Lady. I leaned over and pressed play.

There's a few seconds of Jose talking on his cell phone, pacing back and forth in his store. Tolstoy hits the door first. He zooms in, gun drawn. "Hand me the phone. Gimme the phone," Tolstoy orders.

Lady immediately stiffened, and her brown velvet eyes wid-ened.

"Oh my God, that's him," Lady said. Tears spilled down her cheeks faster than she could wipe them away.

"Are you okay?" Barbara asked, putting her hand across Lady's back.

"My heart is just racing right now," Lady said, starting to tremble. "Just to see him come through that door like that makes me shake all over. It brings back a lot of bad memories."

"Put your hands behind your back," Tolstoy barks to Jose.

"That's him talking right now. I know it," Lady said. His loud and pompous voice was unmistakable.

"You're sure?" Barbara asked. "You're really sure?"

There was no doubt. Shortly after leaving the *Daily News*, Lady contacted internal affairs and the special victims unit to identify Tolstoy as her attacker. "He doesn't deserve to wear the police badge. If he did it to me, he'll strike again," she said.

And yet Tolstoy remained on the street. Barbara and I thought this was mind boggling, indicative of a back-slapping good ol' boys culture in which a cop's word trumps a woman's damning and convincing accusation. At the time, we didn't know that internal affairs had a file on Tolstoy.

Barbara and I went back to the search warrant room. We had little to go on. No names or addresses, just a hunch that we'd find other victims.

We pulled search warrants for raids in which Tolstoy was present, combing through three years' worth. Out of thousands, we set aside at least 150 warrants that listed Tolstoy's badge number.

The warrants gave us the addresses and dates of the raids. To find people, Barbara and I typically used a database that culled information, like home mortgages, liens and bankruptcies, civil suits and voter records, creating thumbnail people profiles. All we had to do was type an address into the database, and names of occupants, both former and current, would pop up. But the women we were looking for lived off the grid. They didn't have landlines, their cell phone numbers changed constantly, and they moved every few months.

Barbara and I would have to rely on old-fashioned shoe leather to find potential Tolstoy victims. The method was inefficient, tedious, and tiresome. We'd often arrive at a house to find the tenants long gone. Other times we'd find the house abandoned, the windows and doors boarded with graffiti-marred plywood. We kept in touch via cell phone, updating each other on our progress—or lack thereof.

Occasionally we went out together, and of course Barbara drove. One afternoon, we turned down a narrow street and found ourselves in the middle of a feud. Two men, each surrounded by their own posse, stood on opposite sides of the street, cursing at each other. One of the men walked over to a parked car and popped the trunk. "I'm gonna get my piece," he said.

"Oh shit. Did he say he's getting his piece?" I said.

"Yeah, we need to get out of here," Barbara said.

That's all we need, to get killed in the crossfire, I thought.

Barbara hit the gas, the car lurched forward, and she sped through the stop sign. "Whoa, Slicey," I cautioned. Barbara stretched her right arm across my chest, like the protective bar on an amusement park ride, as I jammed my hands against the dashboard. We came to a dead stop, stuck behind an idling car parked in the middle of the one-way street. The driver was yapping to a guy on a stoop. This wasn't a part of town where you wanted to beep your horn. We had two choices: wait, or reverse down the street. We waited.

When we finally tracked down people who got raided, they told us a slew of horror stories about the cops. Tolstoy and his squad members splintered doors with battering rams, urinated in bathtubs, poured bleach on family photos, upended couches, and sliced open cushions. The cops ordered pizza or made a McDonald's run and then discarded empty boxes, Styrofoam containers, and food wrappers all over the house. They helped themselves to beer and vodka, drinking straight from the bottle. They spewed venom—"You people live like animals" and "This place stinks like shit." They swiped whatever caught their eye—PlayStations, video games, CDs, jewelry. They always took money and even smashed kids' piggy banks and pocketed coins.

Almost everyone Barbara and I talked to remembered Jeff, the cop they described as "the tall one with the blue eyes." They mostly remembered his lunatic rants. "Get the fuck on the floor. Shut the fuck up!"

Jeff's style was all gangbusters. "He started out with no re-spect," a narcotics cop told us. "He'd say, 'I have pictures of you, if you don't tell me where the drugs are, you'll lose your kids.' He'd lose control. He started with chaos."

But in Jose's video, Barbara and I saw a softer side to Jeff. When the cops raided the store, a boy, roughly twelve years old, was inside.

The cops usher the boy to the front of the store and tell him to put his hands up. He stands with his back to the camera, his hands cupped to the back of his head, elbows out. Dressed in khaki shorts and a lime green shirt, the boy is a statue as an officer searches his pockets for a gun. Jeff approaches the boy and gingerly questions him. "Where do you live at? In the hood?" Jeff asks his name and age, then lightly pats the boy's stomach and tells him to scram.

Barbara and I saw a tenderness there. It was like Jeff was two people.

We were getting a more complete picture of these cops. After each house we visited, Barbara and I made little nota-tions on the search warrant:

> This is a crack house. White girl (messed up) answered door. Didn't want to talk; Mary Lou says the cops found small amount of pot in her house, stole two PlayStations and money; Fat short white guy choked me. I had kid-ney and pancreas transplant, threw me on the floor; Broke ceiling fans, asked me where cash box was, took $1,500, no woman there; Big guy put gun in my face and said what will happen if I pull the trigger.

Between my sleep-deprived mommy brain and Barba-ra's early-onset senility, plus the sheer number of homes, we relied on these scribbled notes to keep track of which doors we'd knocked on and what people had to say about the raids.

At least a dozen women told us that Tolstoy and the other cops in his squad had degraded and demeaned them.

A forty-eight-year-old woman named Denise described Tolstoy's modus operandi. The cop, whom she described as white and stocky with brown hair, took her alone to an upstairs bedroom. "What's your chest size?" the officer asked, eyeing up Denise's generous breasts in her low-cut white summer dress. Denise gave him lip and more than a little attitude: "What has that got to do with anything?" With that, the cop backed down and didn't touch her.

In another summertime raid, a thirty-year-old woman was asleep, naked, when the cops whooshed into her bedroom. She sat up, startled, gripping the bedcovers to her chest.

"I'm not dressed. I'm not dressed," she shouted, but an officer, whom she described as white with a big belly, scruffy brown hair, and a small goatee, yanked the sheets from her fingers so viciously that she thought he was going to rape her. The woman reached for her clothes and turned to dress with her back to the cops, but the officer who pulled off the covers ordered her to face them. She stood naked before them. She was so terrified that she put her clothes on inside out. The cops sent her downstairs, and she heard them cackling in her bedroom. After they left, she found her personal items, including the couple's sex toys, strewn around the room. They removed a black leather teddy from a drawer and laid it out on top of her dresser. The whole scene frightened her. The cops arrested her thirty-five-year-old husband for giving a few of his prescription painkillers to a friend. The couple lived in Cop Land, a term Barbara and I used to refer to the section of Philadelphia that many police officers, firefighters, and other city employees called home. The woman and her husband weren't drug dealers; they were hardworking middle-class people, and the raid humiliated and wounded them. They felt such shame.

"I'll never get that day out of my head," the woman told me. "Ever since this happened, I don't sleep. I'm not comfortable in my house. . . . I felt like all my dignity had been stripped from me."

Barbara and I were disturbed and repulsed by the cops' behavior. Nothing pissed us off more than men in power who preyed on vulnerable women, and on a Friday night in May, Barbara would meet yet another Tolstoy victim.

25

BARBARA STOOD IN THE CENTER OF A
WEARY BLOCK OF THAYER STREET IN
WEST KENSINGTON, WHERE THE ACID
OF THE DRUG TRADE HAD EATEN AWAY
at its core. A pair of sneakers dangled from
a utility wire that sagged from one side of
the street to the other, probably a signpost,
placed by dealers, to let junkies know that
crack was sold here and to mark the block
as theirs. Barbara could roll her foot over a
drift of litter and find quarter-size drug baggies obscured by sticky soda cans, broken
beer bottles, and Chinese takeout menus.

Tolstoy's squad had raided at least five
homes on this block. Every single one was
now boarded, some with plastic tarps covering glassless second-story windows.

Abandoned homes were a pox on neighborhoods like this. There were some 40,000
vacant homes or lots in Philadelphia, and
the drug war nudged that number higher.
Under state forfeiture laws, the city district

attorney's office had the power to seize drug homes, which then sat empty for months, even years. Drug addicts weaseled through plywood to make crack dens or shooting galleries. Stray dogs and cats took refuge in basements with dirt floors and rodents burrowed into soggy drywall. Neighbors on either side struggled to keep the scourge at bay.

Barbara took in the decay around her—slumped roofs on the verge of collapse, crumbled brick facades, rotted wooden porches, and missing front steps. It was around seven on a Friday night, and Barbara, tired and beaten down, called me. I was at my desk, flipping through Tolstoy search warrants in a manila folder marked "cases w/potential."

"Wendy, I'm on Thayer, and these houses are boarded," she said. "I don't know how we're going to find these people."

"Just come on back. It's getting dark," I said.

For eight weeks now, Barbara and I had been out knocking on doors. Winter had given way to spring, and summer was almost here. Each night, we went home sweaty and dirty. Our clothes and hair reeked of cigarette smoke and household insecticide, and our legs were pocked with flea bites. One night, I tossed my work bag on the stone-tiled porch and a plump cockroach crawled out. I yelped and stomped it to death.

Barbara wasn't ready to give up on Thayer Street. "I'm already here. Let me try a couple more neighbors," she told me.

Barbara climbed the steps to a rickety and cluttered porch, haphazardly covered in green outdoor carpeting. The man who opened the door was short, with a pencil mustache and ink-black hair, slicked back into curls at the nape of his neck. His name was Angel Castro, and he warmed quickly to Barbara. He vividly recalled the raid at the house next door.

In a raid led by Tolstoy, the cops stormed into Angel's

neighbors' house looking for marijuana. Soon after the cops left, a woman emerged; she stood sobbing on her porch.

"Are you okay?" Angel asked softly from his adjoining porch.

"No," she said. Little by little, Angel coaxed details from her. "An officer touched my breasts. . . . He was feeling up on me. . . . He rubbed up on me."

Barbara got excited. "Oh, Angel. Do you know her name? Do you know where she lives now? Can you help me? Please, I have to find her."

Her name was Dagma Rodriguez, and Angel thought he might be able to trace her whereabouts through friends and relatives. "Let me make some calls," he said, and Barbara took a seat next to him on the porch. About an hour later, Angel had an address.

Barbara leaped up and hugged him, then bolted to the car, where she called to tell me, rapid-fire, what Angel had told her. "Can you believe it? I'm telling you, Wendy, we're going to find this woman." I gave Barbara directions to Dagma's house.

There was no way I was going home until I heard back from Barbara. I sat at my computer and gnawed at the jagged skin around my fingernails. Most everyone had gone home for the weekend, but the light was still on in Michael Days's office. I ran through the newsroom and breathlessly flew through his door. "Michael! I'm so excited . . ."

Barbara pulled up at Dagma's house ten minutes later. Dagma's cousin cracked open the door and said Dagma wasn't home; she was out with her fiancé and would be back later that night. Barbara explained why she wanted to talk to Dagma. "Do you mind if I wait for her? I'll just be out here. In my car."

Barbara sat in the dark and thought about Tolstoy. She felt for Dagma and knew what it was like to feel violated. When Barbara was in high school, a boyfriend had tried to force himself on her. She cried no and shoved him away. "You're cold. You're just a prude. No one will ever love you," he sneered.

Dagma arrived home in an old beat-up Chevy. "A reporter is here to talk to you," Dagma's cousin told her as she stepped out of the car. "She wants to know what happened during the raid."

Dagma walked slowly toward Barbara, as if in a trance. Barbara thought Dagma was tentative and leery; she wasn't sure the woman would want to talk about the raid. Then Dagma held out her arms and embraced Barbara. She clutched Barbara tightly for a few long seconds. Dagma stepped back, wiped a tear from her cheek, and said something that Barbara would never forget: "I've been praying for this day."

Dagma recounted the dinnertime raid. It was a tale that would make Barbara despise Tolstoy.

Dagma's fiancé, Armando, was cooking rice and beans and frying chicken drumsticks on the stove when Tolstoy and eight other cops slammed open the front door. "What are you doing—killing cats?" one cop said.

When a cop, whom Dagma would later identify as Jeff, saw the family's pit bull, Goldie, he yelled, "Get the fucking dog out of here before I shoot it."

The cops flipped over the futon couch, ripped a closet door off its metal hinges, and tossed clothes, CDs, everything they had, on the floor. "Where's the fucking gun? Where's the fucking drugs!"

Tolstoy almost immediately spied Dagma, who stood in the living room wearing a lime-green nightgown over a pair of gray sweatpants. He cornered her: "Do you have any tattoos? Let's talk."

Dagma's three kids—ages fifteen, nine, and eight—were outside on a porch of splintered wood planks. The cops had threatened to board her house, take her kids, and throw her out in the street.

Tolstoy led her upstairs. He told her everything would be all right. He just wanted to talk. Dagma inched away from the beefy cop. They were alone in a back bedroom. The room was dark, cavelike, with just a glint of light from a shattered windowpane.

She placed one foot behind her, then the other, and pressed her back against the faded blue wall. Her palms, slick with sweat, fluttered against the cracked plaster. He moved closer. She felt his breath on her face.

"You know you got some big tits," he said. "What size are you? Can I touch them?"

"Please, please, no," she whimpered.

Tolstoy stood cocksure, his bay window of a belly thrust out. She saw a rabid look in his brown eyes.

"Can you show them to me?"

"No. No."

The thirty-three-year-old woman began to cry, tears streaking her smooth brown face framed by coils of long dreadlocks. She folded her hands and clasped them over her breasts. Her heart felt jammed in her throat, choking her. She feared she'd vomit.

"Don't cry. Shhh. Sshhh. Shut up. Be quiet."

She fell to her knees.

"Get up."

"I'm nervous, and I got heart problems. I need my heart pills," she said.

"C'mon. Get up. Get up!" He yanked her up by the elbows and pinned her against the wall.

Oh my God, he's gonna rape me, she thought.

He plunged his hands into the top of her nightgown. His thick fingers slithered under her beige bra. He rubbed her nipples, thumbs moving in circles.

She grabbed his wrists, her hands trembling, and cried louder.

"Shut the fuck up!" Tolstoy yelled.

Now, as he forcefully groped her breasts, she had no way to escape.

"I'm scared. I'm so scared," she told him.

"You don't have to be scared. Scared of what?"

Downstairs, the other narcotics cops noticed he was missing. They knew the deal.

A cop, whom Dagma described as tall and handsome with blue eyes, came halfway up the steps. "Is everything all right?" he called out.

Tolstoy took his hands from Dagma's breasts.

"Yeah. Everything's all right. We're about done here."

He stepped back, a smirk on his face. She slid down the wall and crumpled to the floor, wheezing and gulping.

Tolstoy paused in the doorway and looked back at her.

"Take your shit pills."

26

DAGMA'S STORY WAS UNIMPEACH-
ABLE. FOR STARTERS, SHE'D TOLD HER
FIANCÉ WHAT TOLSTOY DID TO HER
DURING A PHONE CALL TO THE JAIL,
where Armando was locked up after the
cops found three marijuana joints in his
pockets and a rusty, unloaded hunting rifle
inside the Thayer Street house.

"I went off. I was in jail, and there was
nothing I could do but punch the walls. All
I could think of was that he could go back
and do something more," Armando told us.

Next, there was Angel, who consoled
Dagma as she cried on the porch.

Lastly, on the night of the raid, Dagma
went to the nearest police district. She was
hysterical and shaken. "I'm here to make a
complaint against this cop who came to my
house." An officer who spoke Spanish took a
statement.

An internal affairs investigator later
came to Dagma's house. He wanted to bag

her nightgown, bra, and sweatpants as evidence, but Angel advised her not to turn over the clothes. Angel thought it unwise for her to part with the only physical evidence she had. Angel and Dagma's guardedness was symptomatic of a pervasive lack of trust between the community and police. Of course, the police department didn't help mend the rift.

Internal affairs showed Dagma a photo array of some eighty cops. The photos were headshots of uniformed cops. Most dated back years, likely taken when they first joined the force, and Dagma didn't recognize Tolstoy among all those baby-faced cops. "I felt like they were hiding him," Dagma said.

Tolstoy had assaulted Lady four months earlier. But unlike Dagma, Lady didn't file a police complaint immediately after the raid; she went to internal affairs after Barbara and I knocked on her door. Dagma's single complaint, coupled with an inability to identify her attacker, wasn't enough for internal affairs to restrict Tolstoy to a desk.

That all changed on October 16, 2008, when internal affairs yanked Tolstoy off the street. In the six months between Dagma's complaint and October 16, Tolstoy did something that got him red-flagged.

Police sources told us that Tolstoy had engaged in "sexual misconduct," and Barbara and I were almost positive that the incident was connected to the woman Benny had told us about, the woman who'd been fisted.

Benny thought the assault had happened near Torresdale and Orthodox Streets. Barbara and I pulled out a map, zeroed in on the intersection, and pressed "enlarge" on the Xerox machine, tapping the button until it reached 150 percent. We printed out two copies on eleven-by-seventeen paper and drew a fifteen-square-block radius in yellow highlighter.

We circled the intersection with a navy blue Sharpie. We left the office with folders crammed with search warrants for raids on homes within the area's zip code—19124.

We went together; of course Barbara drove. Karl had bought me a GPS for Mother's Day, but Barbara, who sometimes got lost while jogging around her own neighborhood, still managed to get all turned around. "Recalculating route," the GPS girl crooned in a calm, robotic voice. We heard her voice so often that we gave her a name—Henrietta. I wanted to throw the thing out the window.

Torresdale and Orthodox was a wide intersection with bus lanes. There was a pizza shop on one corner and a bodega across the street, next to an appliance store, where each morning the employees dragged used washers and dryers and fridges and stoves out onto the sidewalk, lining them up at curb's edge. There were several car-repair shops and a seedy gentlemen's lounge.

We split up the search warrants and fanned out on foot. In between knocking on doors, we ran down every woman we saw on the street. We ambushed them as they stepped off the bus, emerged from a shop, or ambled along the sidewalk, some with kids in strollers. We asked them if a cop had ever touched them inappropriately, and we were surprised by the number of women who, without hesitation, started off, "Oh yeah. There was this time when . . ."

They recounted chilling stories about a vice squad cop or district cop, or a cop who didn't fit Tolstoy's description. They'd say his name was John or Bill. Some said they'd never been sexually assaulted, but they had a friend or an acquaintance . . .

We had so many tips that Barbara and I didn't know which ones to chase. Some led us miles outside of the 19124 zip code. Because the women weren't sure whether the victim they knew had been "fisted" by a cop, we thought we had to find out—so we could at the very least rule her out. We even asked the women who had supplied the tips to drive around with us while they scanned the streets for the victim they described.

One description was of a white woman with blond, dirty blond, or mousy brown hair and a butterfly tattoo on her shoulder—or maybe her wrist. Barbara and I chased tattooed women down the street, trying to get a closer look.

We began to question whether the incident was even connected to a raid. What if Tolstoy had assaulted this woman somewhere out on the streets? Maybe she was a prostitute. Torresdale and Orthodox was a short 2.3-mile drive from the ground zero of lost souls, an area known as K&A—short for Kensington and Allegheny Avenues, where blow jobs went for $20 and full-on sex in a car or alley was just $10 more.

We spent hours talking to drug-addicted prostitutes with rotten teeth and scabbed faces and arms, the result of obsessively picking at their skin while high on crack. They wobbled around on rail-thin legs, wearing rhinestone-studded stilettos and miniskirts or worn-out Chuck Taylors and low-rise jeans. All had glazed eyes and vacant expressions.

"Are you ladies from the church?" a waiflike woman came up and asked us. Candace had an angelic face—catlike blue eyes, high cheekbones, and dirty blond hair pulled up in a ponytail. She was almost twenty-eight, though she looked no more than twenty. She was drug-worn but beautiful. In her fist, she clutched a wad of bills. She told us she desperately wanted to get clean; she wanted to be able to care for her four-year-old son. I gave her my card. A cop arrested Candace for drug possession a few days later, and she wrote me a letter from jail. "Ms. Ruderman, I honestly need help once return-ing home. My mom reminds me her home is not my home, due to my addiction . . . I do not want to repeat that lifestyle of drugs and prostitution. I write to you with hope of direc-tion. I therefore have no one else to turn to." She included a postscript, "PS, one day maybe you can write a story of my success."

I wrote her back and contacted a social worker who met with Candace in jail. Four days after Candace got released, and two months after we met her, Candace was dead of an overdose. It was heartbreaking.

Barbara and I grew frustrated, yet not discouraged. We decided to track down pimps, thinking it would be an easier and more efficient method to find a hooker who'd been vic-timized. We guessed that a prostitute might confide in her pimp.

A lot of the pimps we met didn't fit the stereotype. One was toothless and frail, in his sixties, and suffering from diabetes-related foot ulcers; another was a former hooker turned mother hen in her fifties. She had large, saggy breasts and wiry, broomlike gray hair.

She suggested we find a pimp named Omar, who had a stable of hookers, but she warned us that he was violent, possi-bly dangerous, known to smack his girls around.

I took one side of Kensington Avenue; Barbara took the other. The El trains whistled and click-clacked overhead. Bar-bara found one of Omar's hookers outside a mini-mart. The girl was skittish and her eyes shifted around in the sockets, chameleon-like. She gestured with her head toward me. "See that short little woman with the glasses . . ."

I was on the other side of the street, talking to a black man wearing a white knit skullcap, even though the temperature was pushing eighty. He sat on a concrete step, his back against a reddish brown door.

"Hi, I'm looking for Omar," I said. "Do you know him?"

"Yeah, I know him."

He was friendly, a bit of a jokester, and we started to chit-chat. Somehow we got on the subject of our favorite movies. We both liked films about police corruption, like *Serpico*. Laughing, I handed him my card and asked him to pass it on to Omar.

Barbara rushed toward me, crossing the street against the light. "What did he say?"

I was puzzled by her excitement. "He said he'd tell Omar we were lookin' for him."

"Wendy. That was Omar. You were talking to Omar."

I looked back, and he was gone. He'd slipped behind the reddish door. We knocked, and no one answered. I tugged on the handle, but the door was locked.

I got home, and Karl was watching a home-remodeling show on the DIY Network. My escape was work; his was fantasizing about projects that never got done. He was adorable, with those damn Bambi eyes and heart-shaped lips that broke into a gigantic smile. I leaned in and kissed him.

"How was work?"

"I spent all day looking for a pimp named Omar."

Karl put his hand up. "Please, I don't want to know. Don't tell me."

Barbara and I could do crazy. We understood crazy.

We both came from zany Jewish families that instilled a strong, often obsessive and neurotic work ethic. Karl summed up the Ruderman motto as "Work till you drop, then go out to a restaurant." I was surprised Karl, who came from a re-served Catholic family, married me.

A few months before our wedding, Karl went with my family on a trip to Martha's Vineyard. It was my mom's idea to go to a bathing-suit-optional beach. She stripped naked, wearing only sneakers and white tube socks, and slathered sunscreen all over her body. Karl averted his eyes. "Take a good look," she told Karl. "See these raisin boobs—this is what Wendy will look like in thirty years."

Barbara's mom was a rebel. Instead of settling down with a nice Jewish boy, she fell in love with a smooth-talking British goy. When the couple married, Barbara's grandmother sat shivah and threatened suicide; she refused to meet her daughter's new husband, never even spoke his name. Years ago, Barbara's dad worked on a cruise line, entertaining elderly women. He later described his job title as "cruise ship gigolo." Barbara wasn't sure he was joking.

People like Omar had nothing on Barbara's dad and my mom. Now, *they* were scary; they were uncorked and unfiltered, and Barbara and I were sometimes more afraid of what would fly out of their mouths than of getting hurt—or killed—while in pursuit of this mystery woman. But we also feared failure—and at times, that fear blinded us.

"You're putting this story ahead of your own safety," Hutch told Barbara. "You're losing touch with reality. You're all consumed with this story, but you're gonna knock on a door and get assaulted, raped, or robbed."

Hutch worried constantly about Barbara and gave her unsolicited advice on how to stay safe. Some of his suggestions made sense—carry Mace and step back, out of reach, after knocking on a stranger's door. Of course she did neither. Hutch also doled out advice that made us chuckle. "Before you go out, call the district cops, tell them you're a reporter for the *Daily News* and let them know where you are and what you're doing, and see if they can send someone by to check on you."

I worked so much that when I headed out one morning, Brody smirked and said, "Mom, it was so nice having you for a visit." He knew how to twist the knife.

When Karl went shopping or out for a jog, Sawyer asked, "Mom, are you babysitting us?"

I had largely relinquished my parenting role to Karl, but I still wanted control. I left Karl notes on the refrigerator or front door: "Don't forget to give Brody and Sawyer fruit." "Brush their teeth." "Make them eat carrots." I often added, "I love you," so Karl wouldn't be too mad.

Karl began to talk about getting a vasectomy, and I suspected that he wanted to get snipped just so he could veg on the couch for a weekend and get a break from the kids.

Barbara and I realized we were driving the people in our lives nuts, but we just couldn't stop. We kept coming back to the same search warrant. A raid that took place on October 16, 2008—the exact date Tolstoy was pulled from the street.

27

IT WASN'T JUST THE DATE ON THE SEARCH WARRANT THAT DREW OUR ATTENTION; IT WAS THE ADDRESS. THE COPS RAIDED AN APARTMENT—ON ORTHODOX STREET.

The apartment wasn't anywhere close to Torresdale, but Barbara and I had a strong feeling that this particular raid was key to our search for the woman. We repeatedly swung by the apartment. Sometimes we went together, other times separately. Each time no one was home, and we left business cards and notes, only to find them still jammed in the door seam when we returned.

The search warrant offered scant details. The cops were looking for a drug dealer named Beamer, whom they believed sold crack out of the apartment. During the 7:45 p.m. raid at the apartment, the cops found a gun and drugs, but they couldn't arrest Beamer because he wasn't home and they didn't know his real name.

"Beamer." That was all we had to go on.

Beamer no longer lived there, so Barbara and I canvassed the blocks around his old apartment, asking if anyone knew where we could find him.

The neighborhood was in the heart of a once-robust retail mecca of family-owned pharmacies, hardware stores, diners, florists, and shoe and clothing shops. The shopping district started to lose its luster in the late 1990s, when dollar stores and cash-for-gold pawnshops elbowed out the charm.

Despite the area's decline, many of the homes, including Georgian-style structures built in the late 1700s, retained their grace. Most homes were boxy free-standing, three-story twins separated by alleys. From the street, Barbara and I could see the Philadelphia skyline in the distance.

By now, a lot of the people we approached on the street knew who we were. All we had to do was mention *Daily News* and police corruption and they'd say, "Ohhh! You're the ones doing Tainted Justice." They were eager to help and loaded us up with first names of women who had lived in Beamer's apartment building: Latifa, Kia, Keiana, Tonya, Dashay, and Nicole.

Barbara and I were convinced that Beamer had some kind of connection to this woman. To find him was to find her. But no one seemed to know where Beamer had moved.

Then on a warm, sunny afternoon, I met Shante. When I first approached her as she sat on a front stoop, I wasn't sure if she was a man or a woman. Her head was shaved, and she reminded me of a black Sinead O'Connor. She wore knee-length jean shorts, brown Timberland boots, and a wife-beater, or ribbed white tank top, that showed off her muscular biceps.

Shante was a twenty-one-year-old convicted drug dealer,

openly gay, with a sexy, raspy voice. She'd been locked up at least six times, beginning at age sixteen, when she was found guilty of attempted murder in a bloody shootout. Shante's street name was Pop, and Barbara and I wondered if the nickname sprang from the shooting, though Shante claimed Pop was a reference to her old soul ways. She was fiercely loyal to family and friends, a street lioness who protected and provided for her loved ones.

On her Facebook page, she posted photos of herself holding wads of cash, getting high, and wearing designer Air Jordans. Shante was proud of her plum-shaped lips and poked fun at her gut, calling herself "fatboy shit."

Tattoos covered Shante's neck, upper chest, arms, and hands. The designs were rudimentary, inked in one color, either black or navy. Some of Shante's tattoos were the work of a guy named Skinny who made house calls, like the Fuller Brush man. Shante wanted to get rid of a tattoo that read DANGER. "This is gone," Shante said, rubbing her neck. "It was a girl I used to mess with." Two teardrops, tattooed in black ink, were etched under her left eye, just above her cheekbone. On her right arm she sported a tattoo of comedy-tragedy theater masks, with the words GOOD GIRL BAD GIRL. That about summed her up.

Shante not only knew Beamer, they were close friends, and she had his cell number programmed into her phone. She wouldn't give me Beamer's number, but she promised that she'd tell him we were looking for him. When I didn't hear from Shante, I called her—a lot. "I'm so sorry. I know you must think I'm the biggest pest, but . . ."

A week or so later, late in the evening, I called Shante yet again. She picked up, and I could hear music and laughing in the background. She sounded giddy, and I wondered if she was high. I took a deep breath. "Shante, I haven't heard from Beamer yet. Can you please just give me his number?" To my amazement, she did.

Barbara offered to call Beamer, and I agreed that was a good idea. Barbara had a knack for cracking tough nuts. She could have broken Al Capone.

But each time she tried Beamer's number, no one answered, and Barbara decided to stop by Beamer's old apartment for the fourth time. A teenage girl answered the door, called her mom at work, and handed Barbara the phone. The girl's mom was furious. "Listen, I'm tired of you and that other reporter coming around here. I told the police the same thing—'The woman doesn't live here anymore. I don't know who she is, and I don't know where she went.' Just leave us alone."

Barbara zoomed back to the office. "Wendy, this has got to be the right place. The cops had been there. They were looking for a woman." We decided to play our last card. Barbara called a source on the FBI–internal affairs task force. Barbara knew to ask a narrow question, one with a yes or no answer. This way, the source wouldn't feel too exposed.

"I'm going to give you three addresses. All you have to do is tell me if the address is familiar to you. Okay," Barbara asked.

"Okay," the source said.

Barbara gave him the Orthodox Street address first. "Yes," he said, "that's familiar."

The task force was looking for the woman, too, and at this point, the source figured Barbara and I might have a better chance of finding her. He knew we were tenacious; he also knew that people on the street often felt more comfortable talking to us than to police investigators.

"If you find her, can you try to convince her to contact us?" the source asked, and Barbara agreed.

Beamer. Beamer. Beamer. We had to find him. I was giving up hope. It was about 8:30 on a Friday night. I rolled a chair next to Barbara, and she dialed Beamer's number. I heard a muffled hello, and Barbara stiffened and gripped my arm. I clenched both my fists and pumped them up and down, wearing an alligator smile. Go, go, go, go, Barbara. C'mon, c'mon, do it.

"I'm soooo happy to finally talk to you. You just don't know," Barbara cooed, her moss-colored eyes bulging as she glanced at me and nodded like a bobblehead.

Barbara explained that she was looking for a woman who'd been sexually assaulted by a cop during the raid at his apartment. "We know he's done this to other women. . . . This is your chance to do the right thing and see justice."

I rolled my eyes. Barbara stopped talking, and Beamer said he'd help us. He knew the woman and thought he might see her over the weekend. He promised to call Barbara back.

"Thank you. Thank you so much, Beamer," Barbara gushed. "You're my hero."

I gently punched Barbara in the arm. She was incorrigible. I later teased Barbara about her new hero after we learned that Beamer was a twenty-eight-year-old pimp who ran a brothel.

Because Barbara had been editor for a few years, the *Daily News* hadn't given her a work cell and she hadn't thought to ask for one. So she used her personal phone for the Tainted Justice series. But now this was becoming a problem. Unfamiliar numbers popped up on Barbara's cell at all hours. She was never sure whether the caller was a pimp, drug dealer, crackhead—or a suitor from Match.com.

Barbara kept her phone within earshot all weekend, even while gardening or bathing. At a dinner party, Barbara placed her phone in front of her on the table. "I'm really sorry. I'm expecting an important call from Beamer." Her friends just looked at her.

He never called. Early Monday morning, Barbara couldn't take it anymore. She paced around her back deck and dialed his number. "Yeah, I talked to her," Beamer said casually. "She's really scared, but . . ."

Beamer gave Barbara the woman's first name—we'll call her Naomi—and her number.

Barbara called me right away. "Wendy, Beamer came through. My hero came through," she said, tickled with delight.

28

NAOMI AGREED TO MEET WITH BAR-
BARA AND ME, BUT SHE WAS PETRI-
FIED OF THE COPS, TERRIFIED THAT
TOLSTOY AND HIS CRONIES WOULD
harm her if she talked. We picked her up
about a block from her new apartment. She
slipped into the backseat and slid down, ob-
scuring the side of her face with her right
palm. Barbara drove us out of the area.

Naomi was twenty-four and eight months
pregnant with her fourth child. She sup-
ported her kids—ages four, two, and one—
and her out-of-work father with a part-time
job at a child day care and help from
public assistance. Her black hair, which
she straightened, fell like a smooth, velvety
sheet down her back. A thick curtain of
bangs stopped just above her eyes, the color
of coffee beans. She was reticent by nature,
her emotions enclosed within eggshell-thin
walls. She had a regal air about her.

Naomi had been living on Orthodox

Street for about a month when the cops raided the apartment building. Beamer wasn't her pimp or her boyfriend; he was her landlord, or so she thought.

She had bumped into Beamer, an acquaintance, on the street while looking for a place to live. Beamer was a slickster who never missed an opportunity to make some extra cash. The tenants who had lived on the second floor got evicted, and the apartment sat empty. Beamer, who lived in the first-floor apartment, masqueraded as the building's landlord and duped Naomi into paying him $200-a-month rent for a room upstairs. She was essentially a squatter, though she didn't realize it at the time.

Barbara and I offered to take her to lunch. Naomi picked a hole-in-the-wall pizza joint where she ordered a single slice, eating only a few bites, and no drink.

She spoke in whispers, recounting in a flat, detached voice what Tolstoy had done to her, as if the assault had happened to a stranger.

The night of October 16 was unseasonably warm, and Naomi was getting ready for a night out with her live-in boyfriend, Raheem. Naomi's kids were spending the night at her mom's house. She stepped out of the tub and began to towel off. Suddenly, a loud boom from the downstairs apartment rattled the floor beneath her, and Naomi flinched. The sound startled her, and she quickly dressed, pairing a pink and white spaghetti-strap top with a mini jean skirt. Her skin still warm from soapy bathwater, Naomi walked to the stairwell and inched gingerly down the steps to see what was going on. One after the other, cops powered upstairs toward her.

The cops ordered Naomi and Raheem to go to the first floor, where they cuffed them with plastic restraints. The couple couldn't understand why the cops were there, and so many of them—ten in all.

"Where are the drugs?" one cop yelled.

"We don't have any drugs," Naomi replied.

"Where's this guy Beamer?" a cop asked.

"I don't know. We're just renting a room from him," she explained.

Naomi noticed Tolstoy eyeing her up and down. There was something sinister about him.

"I need to talk to you upstairs," Tolstoy told her.

Tolstoy directed her to the steps and she complied, with him following closely behind. Raheem, who stayed downstairs with the other cops, lost sight of her.

"Look. We're not doing anything wrong," she warily told Tolstoy, her hands restrained behind her back, as she treaded upstairs. "Really. We don't have any drugs."

"Be quiet," he said. She sensed frustration in his tone. "I just want to talk to you. I'm just going to ask you more questions, and then I'll take off the handcuffs."

They reached the landing, and Tolstoy freed her hands. They stood in the doorway of her apartment.

"You know anyone in the area who sells crack cocaine?"

"No, Officer."

"You sure you have nothing in your room?"

"I have nothing, Officer. I'm sure."

"Well, I have to see for myself."

She told him he could look all over the apartment; she had nothing to hide. She expected Tolstoy to ransack her room, but he didn't.

"I'm gonna need to see under your shirt."

"But I have no bra on."

"That's OK," Tolstoy said.

She asked if he could send up a female officer. Tolstoy ignored her request.

"You know I could lock you up for the drugs we found downstairs."

Naomi knew that made no sense, but she was too scared to argue. Her hands quivered as she slowly lifted up her pink and white top. Not saying a word, Tolstoy's meaty hands clasped her breasts with his fingers moving in a caressing squeeze.

"Lift up your skirt," he told her.

Naomi again asked for a female officer, and Tolstoy again threatened to lock her up for drugs that weren't hers.

Naomi gripped the denim and slowly lifted the skirt up.

"I have to see in your underwear."

Naomi tugged her panties down just slightly, just enough to show him she had nothing hidden there. Tolstoy lurched forward and yanked her panties down further.

"Please. I don't feel comfortable with that," she begged.

"Be quiet."

Tolstoy jammed his index and middle fingers into her vagina. He thrust them inside her with a violent jab. Naomi turned her head to the side, avoiding his face. If I don't look at him, I won't feel anything, she thought.

Naomi winced at the pain. She could feel the burn, the sting as she began to bleed.

She backed up, trying to pull away from him. She reached down and tried to pull up her panties with one hand and push down her skirt with the other.

"I don't want you touching me like that," she whimpered.

"I'll have to put you back in handcuffs."

"Stop," she cried. "Stop."

He grabbed her shoulders with such force that the spaghetti strap of her shirt broke off.

Tolstoy's expression changed instantly. His eyes became saucer-like. He looked flustered, almost fearful.

"If they ask you how your strap broke," he told her, "you tell them you always tie it, and it just came loose."

After the cops left, Raheem went upstairs to find Naomi. The first thing he noticed was her torn shirt, then the terror in her eyes. She told him she was bleeding, that the cop hurt her, maybe scratched her or caused internal damage.

They walked almost a mile to the nearest hospital where Naomi gave the staff a false name—Asia Johnson. Naomi was vague with the details.

"I just want to get myself checked out. I just feel funny down there," she told nurses. "I just want to make sure I'm okay." She was too embarrassed to say exactly what Tolstoy did, but nurses suspected immediately that she'd been sexually assaulted.

"I know there's something going on," a nurse gently told her.

The staff called uniformed cops to escort Naomi and Raheem to another hospital, where the special victims unit was located. Nurses ordered a rape kit and alerted SVU investigators, who bagged her ripped shirt and underwear as evidence, and told her they'd run DNA tests. Naomi pulled aside a female officer. "My name's not Asia Johnson," she whispered. "I made up the name because I was scared."

Naomi didn't know Tolstoy's name. But internal affairs had more than a hunch. Dagma had made a similar complaint six months earlier, and at the time she, too, couldn't identify Tolstoy by name. But in both cases, Tolstoy was the only cop who had been alone with the women.

So internal affairs took Tolstoy off the street the same night that Naomi showed up at the special victims unit.

Two days after the assault, Naomi was walking down the sidewalk near her apartment when two uniformed cops pulled their police car to the curb beside her. The cop on the passenger side rolled down his window and asked her what happened in her apartment.

"Nothing happened," she said, hoping they'd drive off and leave her alone.

"We've got some information . . . ," the cop began. She ignored him, turned around, and walked off. The cop leaped out of the car, thrust her arms behind her back, handcuffed her, and threw her in the back of the cruiser.

Naomi insisted that this cop was Tolstoy, but Barbara and I couldn't prove it. Tolstoy was on desk duty at the time, but there was a possibility that Tolstoy met up with a cop buddy after work. We knew Tolstoy's squad was chummy with the patrol cops in Naomi's neighborhood. Two district cops had given the squad the initial tip about Beamer dealing crack out of his apartment.

"Whatever you said, take it back," the cop said, all redfaced as he glared at her.

"I don't know what you're talking about," she said.

"You'll be seeing me around," he warned. Then he let her go.

Naomi ran to a pay phone and dialed her mom, who came to pick her up. Together they went to the police district to file a report. But the officers told Naomi they needed a name of the cop who stopped her.

"Listen. We have thousands of police officers."

Naomi and her mom left, disgusted and frustrated. Naomi moved from her apartment on Orthodox Street to her mom's house in New Jersey. Then the phone calls started. Naomi's cell rang at all hours from restricted or unavailable numbers.

"Drop it."

"Don't say nothing."

"I know where you're at."

"We'll find you."

Naomi suspected the callers were cops. She and her mother changed their phone numbers several times, but the calls continued, and Naomi grew afraid to leave home.

Then one day, roughly five weeks after the raid, two investigators showed up at Naomi's mom's house. They sat the two women down and explained they had some evidence linking an officer to the sexual assault. They wanted Naomi to press criminal charges. She just couldn't do it.

"I wouldn't mind going to court if I knew he was going to get locked up," she said. "I'd go to court, but it's not just him making the phone calls. It's not just him stopping me. I don't want to walk down the street and worry what will happen."

Naomi refused to cooperate, and then she disappeared, moving from her mom's house to another apartment. Internal affairs investigators lost track of her. Without Naomi, they decided they didn't have enough to keep Tolstoy on desk duty. So on January 12, 2009—three months after the assault—Tolstoy was put back on the street.

It wasn't until Lady, Dagma, and Naomi all told similar stories to internal affairs that police superiors felt they had no choice. They couldn't leave Tolstoy out there. On April 2, 2009, Lady went to the special victims unit and internal affairs to name Tolstoy as her attacker. The next month, on May 20, 2009, Tolstoy was put back on desk duty and had to relinquish his service weapon.

"Until we investigate further, we don't want him taking police action. We don't want to expose the city to other accusations or to any liability or risk," internal affairs chief inspector Anthony DiLacqua told us.

Barbara called Lady and Dagma to let them know that Tolstoy was off the street. They were grateful and relieved, though forever traumatized.

"I felt like a pig," Dagma told Barbara. "He made me feel so bad. I felt disgusting. I didn't even want to be touched no more from nobody. I was aggravated with myself. I hated myself that instant because I wish that never would have happened to me. I just wanted to run away where no one can find me and just run, run, and leave everything, everything behind, but it's something that I can't do. I can forgive, but I will never, ever forget."

Tolstoy targeted Dagma, Lady, and Naomi for a reason. Each was beautiful, with smooth skin, full sensual lips, and large brown eyes framed by curly lashes. They were pleasers— soft-spoken, slightly fearful of authority, with no arrest record, the type of women who put the needs of their men and their children before their own. They constantly doubted themselves, but beneath the insecurity, there was a sunniness, an optimism. Lady and Dagma shared an inner strength and resolve that propelled them to allow the *Daily News* to print their full names and photos. Dagma and Lady also agreed to do videos, which we posted online. Even now, when Barbara and I watch the videos, we're moved to tears—awed by their courage.

29

BARBARA AND I SPENT THE FALL
CHASING NEW TIPS ABOUT NARCOT-
ICS COPS GONE ROGUE. WE LOOKED
INTO CLAIMS OF MONEY LAUNDERING,
shady real-estate deals, a $50,000 theft of
drug money from a notorious motorcycle
club, and the blackmailing of prostitutes
who advertised on Craigslist. On each lead,
we ran smack into a dead end.

While we spun our wheels, exhausting
ourselves, the police department moved
forward with reforms. For the first time in
twenty-three years, police brass put out a
new directive that placed tighter controls on
narcotics officers and their confidential informants.

The new regulations spelled out what
narcotics cop could and could not do with
informants. Some of the dos and don'ts on
the list were so obvious they were almost
comical: No sexual relationships. No gifts.
No social, financial, or business dealings.

Police Commissioner Ramsey also appointed a chief integrity officer to scrutinize drug cases that used informants. The reforms recognized that the relationship between a cop and his informant was potentially toxic. Drug informants weren't trustworthy, and corruptible cops couldn't be trusted to work with them, not without close supervision. From now on, all contact between the two, including phone conversations and meetings, had to be documented and reviewed by higher-ups, and a supervisor had to witness all police payouts to informants.

The police department finally got what some of Benny's relatives had been saying all along: as Jeff and Benny grew more dependent on one another, their relationship was poisonous. Jeff earned about $100,000 a year, almost half from court overtime, and he won accolades and commendations for drug arrest numbers that soared—mostly on Benny's back. Benny used some of the money he earned helping to take down dealers to feed his own drug habit. They were addicted to each other.

Barbara and I only came to understand this after we spoke with Susette, the woman Benny called his first wife, and their three adult children—Susette Jr., Benny Jr., and Iesha.

"They were using each other," twenty-six-year-old Benny Jr. said. "But it was like my dad was going down, and Jeff was going up."

Barbara and I sat in Susette's living room, where the family explained that Benny was, and probably always would be, an addict. He liked it all—crack, cocaine, marijuana, and pills.

He'd been in and out of rehab at least four times, and even now, he would pawn almost anything for a fix.

When Susette was in Puerto Rico for her grandmother's funeral, Benny claimed someone broke into their house through a back window and stole a television and Benny Jr.'s

Nintendo, but Susette knew better. When Benny Jr. was fifteen, he bought a new bike with money he earned as a stock boy at a sneaker store, but his father snuck it out of the basement and sold it for crack. Benny Jr. asked his father what happened to his $250 GT bicycle. At first Benny denied knowing anything about it, then he just said, Yeah, I took it. "He didn't give a reason. I already knew," Benny Jr. said. When Susette realized her high school graduation ring and her grandmother's necklace were missing, she forced Benny to tell her what he'd done with them. Susette marched over to the drug dealer's house to try to buy the jewelry back.

Time after time, Benny called Susette from dark, fetid crack dens, where she'd find him sprawled out on a filthy mattress, immobilized by paranoia. "Don't let him back in here," Susette rebuked the dealer as she dragged Benny out to the car. She screamed at him the whole ride home.

"Sorry, Susette. I'll never do it again," he vowed.

She thought, Yeah, right. "Da, da, da . . . I'm not going to get you no more. That's on you."

When the kids were little, Susette covered for Benny. But when they grew older, she wanted them to understand the poison. She dug around in Benny's pockets and fished out a baggie of crack. She sat the kids down at the kitchen table and held the drugs out in her open palm. "This is what your father is doing," she told them. She walked stoically into the bathroom and flushed the drugs down the toilet.

Benny's habit only grew worse after he started working with Jeff. Benny sometimes sampled the drugs during a buy, claiming if he didn't, the dealer might suspect he was a snitch or an undercover cop. At the end of the night, Jeff handed Benny his informant pay and dropped him at a corner near his house, but Benny didn't go home. He disappeared for days.

Susette called Jeff to let him know. "Benny went out and did this for you, and now he didn't come back. He's doing his stuff out there. You know he's snorting coke and smoking crack," she said.

"Nah. Not Benny," Jeff said.

"He's always out there doing stuff with you, and then he gets caught up because he has to try it. He keeps on," she told him.

"He doesn't have to try nothing. Benny comes out and he's perfectly fine," Jeff said.

Jeff either didn't believe her or didn't want to listen.

Benny Jr. called Jeff five times, sometimes crying:

"My dad is on drugs heavy."

"My dad has problems. You have to help my dad."

"You're making my dad worse."

"He's gonna kill himself, or someone's gonna kill him."

Still, Jeff wouldn't listen. He couldn't quit Benny. It was a vicious cycle—Jeff gave Benny money. Benny bought dope and now had a new address to give Jeff. Jeff set up a raid. Benny again got paid. Then Benny scoped out his next crack house. And on it went.

When Benny was off on a binge, he'd sell his sneakers for crack. "It would be a miracle if he'd come back with his shoes on. He'd come back barefoot," Benny Jr. said.

One day, Susette couldn't take it anymore. She wanted him out, but he refused to leave unless she gave him $2,500. "I asked at work about borrowing from my 401k. He went with me to cash the check," said Susette, who worked as a social worker. "Then I started thinking if I gave him the whole thing, I'd be behind. I gave him two thousand dollars and kept five hundred." Benny, who was already running around with Sonia, moved in with her.

For the big moments in the lives of his oldest children,

Benny was a no-show. In 2007, he bought Iesha a $500 dress for her Sweet Sixteen party, but he didn't give her what she wanted most. In front of the some 250 guests, Benny, as her father, was expected to perform a coming-of-age ceremony. Benny was supposed to remove Iesha's flat shoes and replace them with strappy heels to symbolize that she'd become a lady. Iesha cried, her face streaked with mascara, as Benny Jr. stepped in for their dad. He didn't go to her high school graduation, nor did he show for his two oldest kids.

"He was always promising stuff," Benny Jr. told us. "Like 'I'm going to take you to the Phillies game. I'm going to do this. I'm going to do that.' Somehow I would expect it. But after a while, I knew not to expect it."

Benny Jr. tried to act like he didn't care, like he was over it, but he wasn't—clearly. None of them were. They were wounded.

For Benny, being an informant was like having a legal license to do drugs. The police department essentially became Benny's pusher. Cops like Jeff were curbing the drug trade—and at the same time feeding it. When Jeff evicted Benny and deactivated him as an informant, Benny lost a key pipeline to money and drugs.

Barbara and I thought that Jeff might not have known that Benny was an addict. We kept coming back to the fact that Jeff rented a house to Benny. "Would you rent a house to a known crackhead?" Barbara asked me when we wrestled with it in our heads. "You'd have to be crazy." Jeff also helped Benny get jobs with his friends, including current and former cops who had started their own businesses.

Benny never came across, at least not to Barbara and me, as a dope fiend. He was a master at hiding it. Up until Benny burned Jeff, Jeff probably thought he was a good judge of character and knew how to smell a con. I thought the same thing about myself.

Throughout the yearlong Tainted Justice series, Benny was my albatross. He would call me, not Barbara, whenever he had a problem. Barbara and I later speculated that Benny picked me because I had little kids. Brody and Sawyer were around the same age as Benny's two youngest, Giovanni and Gianni. On top of that, I was a pushover around kids, and Benny knew how to play me, knew just the right sob story to spin: he had no heat in the house and the kids got sick from the cold; he and Sonia couldn't afford to give the kids a Christmas; he'd spent what little money he had on Catholic school tuition for Gio.

Benny repeatedly told me, with slight variations, that his kids were suffering in the wake of the *Daily News* story about him. He said Gio didn't understand why the family had to keep moving. "I feel like we're running from place to place," Benny told me, crying. "I feel bad. I should be taking my son to Cub Scouts." Benny said he couldn't risk being seen with the kids. He couldn't walk them to school or take them trick-or-treating without putting their lives in danger. He painted himself as a good parent who was miserable because he couldn't give them a normal childhood or provide for them. He said that every time he tried to get a job, potential employers Googled him and got put off when they came across the *Daily News* story.

Other times Benny called and said he was being followed, convinced that this was the day his body would end up in a ditch. Sometimes Barbara and I believed that the day would come when we'd hear from Sonia, the police, whoever, that Benny was dead and we wondered how we'd live with the guilt. There were plenty of drug dealers who would get freed from prison and want street justice. Revenge and snitch murders were commonplace on Philly's streets.

But those who knew the rules of the hood told Barbara and me that anyone who wanted to off Benny would wait. They would make him sweat, for seven, eight years maybe, knowing that life on the run was no life. And time would protect his killer. Cops would be hard pressed to finger a suspect. There were too many to name, and the cases had grown rusty.

When Benny wasn't talking about his own murder, he claimed he'd kill himself, if not for the kids. "These little guys, they keep me going."

I was tortured by this. I spent hours talking to Benny on the phone, trying to console him while trying to console myself.

"Benny, I'm sorry. I feel like this is my fault."

"No. No. Noooo, Wendy," Benny said, before throwing in that FBI and internal affairs investigators always told him that Barbara and I didn't give a shit about him, we just wanted a story. "I tell them, noooo. Youse girls have been there for me."

Benny did a number on my head, and for the longest time, I couldn't disentangle myself from him. I bought Benny groceries for Thanksgiving and toys for his kids at Christmas and for Gio's birthday. At my weakest moments, Barbara stopped me from giving him money. "Wendy, don't do it." She reminded me that it would be unethical and would cross the line as a journalist; she saved me from myself. Jeff didn't have the same oversight. Jeff allowed himself to get sucked in by the drug trade's riptide, which separated him from his oath as a law enforcement officer.

When Barbara and I left Susette's house, we felt sick. I realized that we weren't to blame for the mess Benny had made of his life. I was done with Benny, done feeling responsible. I was free.

30

NOT SURPRISINGLY, BARBARA AND I DIDN'T MAKE GEORGE BOCHETTO'S CHRISTMAS CARD LIST.

That year Jeff's attorney sent out holiday cards that could only have been dreamed up by this contentious barrister. The card featured a Photoshopped image of Bochetto and his law partner swimming underwater, surrounded by teeth-baring sharks and a bosomy blonde in a skimpy bikini. In the photo, Bochetto's wavy hair floats atop his head and a plume of air bubbles rise up from his nose. He's wearing a ferocious expression and his trademark pinstriped suit, briefcase in hand. The card reads, "Litigation is an ocean . . . full of sharks." The words next to Bochetto and his law partner, Gavin Lentz, say: "Man Eaters . . . George and Gavin wish you an ocean of good fortune in 2010."

A *Daily News* reporter who had received Bochetto's card thought I'd find it humorous and handed it to me. "I love it," I said, as I thrust a pushpin through Bochetto's forehead and tacked it up on the fabric-covered wall divider near my computer.

Barbara and I had moved past Tainted Justice to write stories on topics other than police corruption, and the *Daily News* was nearing the end of its fourteen-month slog through bankruptcy.

Philadelphia Media Holdings, which owned the *Daily News*, the *Inquirer*, and Philly.com, was more than $300 million in debt. Though the company cleared about $15 million in profit in 2009, that gain was gobbled up by $26.6 million in legal and professional fees associated with the bankruptcy. That expense included legal bills generated by the lenders, but paid for by Philadelphia Media Holdings.

The company was now slated for the auction block, where it would be sold to the highest bidder. For months, the auction was held up by a legal battle over credit bidding in federal court: company CEO Brian Tierney and his investment group wanted all the bids in cash; the senior lenders, who held the largest portion of the company's debt, wanted to use that debt as IOUs to bid on the company. Tierney wasn't expected to win the fight, but the US Court of Appeals for the Third Circuit handed him an improbable victory—and the auction was a go.

The victory meant Tierney stood a chance of holding on to the papers. Tierney ramped up his efforts to recruit investors who would go up against senior lenders. He approached every super-rich benefactor or businessman in the region and crisscrossed the country in search of civic-minded bidders. Tierney put it to them straight: This isn't an investment. It's philanthropy. We'd be saving a cultural gem, an institution with a community value that could never be measured in dollars.

This was a change in thinking for Tierney. Like a lot of publishers across the country, Tierney had believed that Internet advertising would save newspapers. He figured if he could drive up web traffic on Philly.com and increase the number of page views, he could charge more for online advertising. But even though the number of page views soared on Philly.com, the Internet became awash with competing websites, which drastically drove down the price of online advertising.

"This aspect of the business really scares the crap out of me," Tierney mused. "You look at it and you say to yourself, 'Online maybe isn't the future.' . . . That was the killer for the model."

Tierney finally realized that newspapers as a for-profit venture were a thing of the past. But that didn't stop him from fighting for his hometown papers, and he mounted a last stand against the lenders in the form of a "Keep It Local" advertising campaign that made them bristle.

"You're in Philadelphia, pal," Tierney said. "This is my town. . . . If this was a box-manufacturing company in Akron, I wouldn't be fighting like this. But I live here."

Tierney cast himself as the home-team backer, and the senior lenders, who included Angelo Gordon, a New York–based hedge fund that specialized in distressed debt, as vultures who would ruthlessly go after short-term dollars and erode the quality of journalism.

Tierney's sales pitch worked, and local investors—the very ones who had lost millions in the first 2006 go-around—once again agreed to put up money, this time sold on the notion that without their help, journalism in Philadelphia would die. The team assembled by Tierney also included new investors: benefactor David Haas, an heir to the Rohm & Haas chemical company fortune; Revlon chairman Ronald Perelman and his philanthropist father Raymond, who together threw in $27 million; and at the last minute, amid the heat of the auction, cable television mogul H. F. "Gerry" Lenfest, who went in for $10 million.

The reality of the impending auction didn't really hit Barbara and me. We were too focused on a fantasy. Barbara and I had already won two national awards for Tainted Justice. The *Daily News* had nominated Tainted Justice for a Pulitzer for investigative reporting, one of the hardest categories to win. Editors at big newspapers across the country nominate reporters every year. Being nominated was nothing more than a pat on the back by your colleagues. It had as much weight as a parent advocating that their kid deserved to be Student of the Year. The *Daily News* wasn't exactly a heavy hitter in Pulitzer world.

We couldn't bring ourselves to say the word, even though there was buzz that we had a shot. Almost every other day, Barbara scooched over to my desk, crouched down until her Cheshire Cat face was at eye level with mine, and began to sway, hands clasped, as if praying or gripped by a stomach cramp. "Wendy," she whispered, "can you imagine if we won the P? Imagine that?"

Any chance of winning would require a little divine intervention. I took out an old photo of my dad. In the photo, I'm no more than fifteen, wearing a sea-green sundress, my long bangs feathered back à la Farrah Fawcett. I'm smiling at the camera, and my dad is gazing at me adoringly. I kissed the image of my dad's face and tucked the photo under my pillow. While out for a jog, Barbara looked to the sky and talked to her mom. "Ma, please, please make this happen . . ."

My dad died in 1997; Barbara's mom died three years later, both of pancreatic cancer. Each was the parent who pushed us to achieve and understood what drove us. Barbara prayed to her mom when she was struggling and grieving over her divorce. I prayed to my dad for help when my three-year-old nephew developed a brain tumor. Barbara and I prayed to them when we wanted something really bad.

At exactly 3:00 p.m. on Monday, April 12, 2010, the winners would be posted on the Pulitzer website, and Barbara and I would know if our break-glass-in-an-emergency parents came through.

The Columbia University Graduate School of Journalism, which administered the Pulitzers, tried to keep the winners a secret until the announcement. A committee of top-tiered editors and journalists from across the country judged the Pulitzers. Committee members often had friends or colleagues at newspapers that submitted Pulitzer entries. Once the committee had whittled down the entries to a few finalists, leaks happened, and winners and finalists got a heads-up.

But on the Friday before the announcement, Barbara and I still hadn't heard anything. We lingered around until about 7:00 p.m., when Michael Days stopped by Barbara's desk on his way out. As the paper's top editor, he'd be the one to get tipped off.

"So I guess you haven't heard anything," Barbara said, looking at him, sullen, with her chin down and her head tilted to the side. Michael shook his head.

"You would have heard something by now, wouldn't you?" Barbara pressed.

"Probably," he said quietly. Michael promised to call her over the weekend if he got any news.

All weekend, Barbara waited for Michael to call. Nothing. By Sunday night, I was depressed. I turned off my cell and went to bed.

The next morning, I debated what to wear to work and whether to break out my contact lenses. I always felt more confident and less bookish without my eyeglasses. I settled on my beat-up ASICS sneakers, $2 black capris from Goodwill, a robin's-egg-blue granny sweater, and saggy cotton undies. I slipped on my glasses. It was my no-win-Pulitzer look, insurance against getting my hopes up. I gave Karl a long squeeze and a kiss.

"Good luck," he said.

"I know we didn't win."

Driving to work, I could barely see out the windshield, which was splattered with purplish white bird droppings, and I couldn't hear the radio over the rumble of my broken muffler. Barbara was just getting out of her car when I pulled into the parking lot. She wore fitted black slacks and a cotton-candy-pink sweater with a matching pink belt.

"I'm sooooo depressed," I said, as I hugged her.

"Me too."

For weeks Barbara and I had nurtured a tiny sprout of hope, and we didn't want that hope to die.

By 2:30 p.m. Barbara had a migraine, and I was holed up in Gar's office while he edited one of my stories. My phone rang.

"Any word?" Karl asked.

"Nope."

I hung up, releasing a puff of air through my lips. "Sorry, that was Karl. He wanted to know if we'd heard anything about the Pulitzer."

Gar seemed taken aback. The *Daily News* had won two Pulitzers in its eighty-five-year history—Richard Aregood won in 1985 for editorial writing, and Signe Wilkinson won for her editorial cartoons in 1992—and both times, Gar and the rest of the newsroom had gotten word ahead of time. Gar had plucked his sapling of hope and tossed it on the compost pile days ago. He had no intention of replanting any seeds until he checked with Michelle Bjork, the assistant managing editor who'd entered our series in the Pulitzer contest.

Gar walked down the corridor to Michelle's office and came back seconds later. "She hasn't heard a thing."

Staring us in the face was Gar's satirical poster, "Despair. It's always darkest just before it goes pitch black." At that moment, I didn't see any humor in it.

"It doesn't matter. This was a great series. These prizes are all politics," Gar said, waving his arm dismissively.

At 2:55 p.m., Michael summoned Barbara and me to a computer in the middle of the newsroom.

"Why does he want us to see that the *New York Times* or the *Washington Post* won?" Barbara muttered in my ear.

"I'm not going over there," I told her.

"We have to. Michael wants us over there."

We walked over to the computer, feeling as if the entire newsroom was about to witness our heartbreak.

31

AT 2:59 P.M., I CHEWED MY NAILS AND
LOOKED DOWN AT THE FLOOR. BAR-
BARA STOOD LIKE A STATUE, ARMS
FOLDED, HER LIPS DRAWN TIGHT. MI-
chael seemed anxious, too. He pressed his
right palm to his cheek. Michelle Bjork sat
at the computer, the Pulitzer website already on the screen. She repeatedly tapped
the refresh button, but the site had yet to be
updated with the 2010 winners.

Then at 3:04 p.m., we heard shouts from
across the room. "Yes! Yes! Yes!" It was Kevin
Bevan, the burly lumberjack-like news editor
who'd coined the phrase "Tainted Justice."

"Yes? Yes?" Michelle called out.

There it was on the computer screen.
"2010 Pulitzer Prize winners: Investigative
Reporting. Barbara Laker and Wendy Ruderman of the *Philadelphia Daily News*."

The newsroom went bonkers. Gasps
exploded into joyful shrieks and raucous
cheers. Barbara and I sprang into the air

like spastic crickets. Barbara's long, honey-colored hair flew upward into a tangled flame, and we bear-hugged Michael, who lifted us off the ground and spun us around. Much of the staff was crying.

Barbara called Josh and Anna, her voice high-pitched in a Minnie Mouse squeak. "I won. We won the Pulitzer."

"I knew it, Mom. I knew you'd do it. I'm so proud of you," Josh said.

I called Karl at home. "We won!"

"You won!"

"Yeah, we won! Get your ass down here!"

Bottles of champagne materialized, followed by the sound of popping corks. Someone handed me an opened bottle of champagne. I looked around for cups and didn't see any, so in a moment of lunacy, I took off my smelly sneaker and poured bubbly into the insole. I gripped the sneaker by the heel, tilted it to my mouth and took a giant swig. It was my tribute to shoe-leather journalism—in a newsroom with no cups.

When Karl arrived, gripping Brody's hand and holding Sawyer on his hip, everyone applauded, and Karl's eyes welled up. They were clapping for him. He had survived a year as a single dad, a year of feeding the kids dinner, giving them baths, putting them to bed, and waiting up for me—often past midnight. I couldn't have won a Pulitzer without his help, and everyone knew it.

Soon, *Inquirer* reporters and editors graciously came down to our newsroom to congratulate us. By then someone had found cups, and the champagne flowed.

The crowd pressed Barbara and me to say a few words, and the room fell quiet. In halting, half-finished sentences, we told everyone that this wasn't just our Pulitzer, it was theirs, too. They had picked up the slack, reporting and writing two or three stories a day so Barbara and I could chase Tainted Justice. "How many papers with thirty people . . . win a Pulitzer," Barbara said shyly, shrinking from the attention.

With that, Michael raised his glass. "It's a great day at the *Daily News.*"

Brian Tierney was at a Newspaper Association of America convention in Orlando when he got the call from Michael. He stood alone in an empty ballroom after a meeting had just broken up. He hung up the phone and stepped into the hallway, where bigwigs from the nation's most prestigious newspapers milled about. He wore a high-wattage grin.

"What's up?" asked a *Washington Post* executive.

"The *Daily News* just won a Pulitzer Prize for investigative journalism," Tierney blurted.

They gathered around, patting him on the back, "Way to go, Bri. Way to go, Brian!"

Tierney later laughed at himself when he realized that most of the newspaper executives congratulating him didn't mention that they, too, had snagged a Pulitzer, though in a different category.

But the *Daily News* was an underdog—the only paper in the country to win a Pulitzer while in bankruptcy. Tierney was on a roll.

"A while back, I was saying that I had this dream we would win at the Third Circuit, then win a Pulitzer, and then we had a good outcome on the auction. . . . Two out of three ain't bad, so, so far, so good," Tierney told *New York Times* media writer David Carr.

About two weeks after we won the Pulitzer, a tense, twenty-nine-hour auction of the newspapers played out at a midtown Manhattan law firm. Tierney and his investment team were holed up in one room, while the creditors were bunkered in another, each camp sleep-deprived, fueled by coffee and emotion, as the bidding war ratcheted up. Tierney's group hit $129 million, and the creditors topped that bid by $10 million. It was soon clear that no matter how much Tierney's group put in, the creditors were going to outbid them.

In the end, the creditors won control of the *Inquirer*, the *Daily News*, and Philly.com for $139 million—roughly one quarter of the $515 million sale price four years earlier. Tierney couldn't believe he'd lost. He turned to his group, his brown eyes and round face bewildered. "That's it? It's over? We're done?"

Tierney felt helpless, just like when he learned his parents had died. "When my mom and dad, both times, when I got a call that they had died, there's that sense when you put the phone down, and you realize there's not a darn thing I can do. There's nobody I can call, there's no, like, 'Oh, let me run there and I can help you.' There was nothing you could do, and this felt the same way."

Tierney boarded a train home from New York City and slumped into a seat. He stared out the window, nursing a Scotch. The train rolled into Philadelphia's Thirtieth Street Station, where Tierney was met by a throng of TV, radio, and print journalists—all looking for a quote to that rote reporter question, "How do you feel?"

"It's been a heck of a fight. . . . We didn't make it. I think I'll go home tonight and sleep like a baby, which means I'll wake up every hour crying," Tierney said, stealing John McCain's line when he lost the 2008 presidential election to Barack Obama.

On May 21, 2010, Tierney sat in his twelfth-floor office for the last time. Feeling spent, he removed his glasses and rubbed his eyes. He packed up his belongings and walked out of the ivory tower on Broad Street.

Three days later, on a drizzling Monday morning, Barbara and I, along with Karl, walked through the gates leading into Columbia University's majestic campus. We climbed the steps to the Low Library, an imposing neoclassical edifice, where the Pulitzers are awarded every year. We walked through the doors, greeted by bronze busts of Zeus and Apollo. Tables draped with white linen and adorned with china plates and wineglasses sat underneath the 106-foot ceiling of the library's rotunda, surrounded by solid green marble columns.

We sat at a table with Michael Days, Gar Joseph, Michelle Bjork—and Brian Tierney. After accepting the award at the podium, we came back to the table, and Tierney stood up. He hugged us and wiped tears from his eyes.

"A beautiful and poetic ending," he said.

The Pulitzer committee cited Barbara and me for "resourceful reporting."

On the cab ride to the train station, I looked over at Barbara and smiled. " 'Resourceful.' *Resourceful*—they got that right, Slime Sista," referring to the nickname bestowed upon us by our cop detractors.

"You think *resourceful* is another word for crazy?" Barbara asked.

We laughed and playfully swatted each other on the arm.

EPILOGUE

AS OF JULY 2013, FOUR YEARS AND FIVE MONTHS AFTER OUR FIRST TAINTED JUSTICE STORY, THE FIVE OFFICERS AT THE CENTER OF THE INVESTIGATION, including Jeff Cujdik And Tom Tolstoy, have not been charged with a crime. All but one, who retired, are still Philadelphia police officers, although they remain on desk duty. They still earn paychecks, paid by taxpayers, and are building up healthy pensions.

The city has paid out almost $2 million to settle thirty-three lawsuits filed by bodega owners and two women who claimed they were victimized by these officers. In settling the cases, the city did not admit any liability.

The FBI has refused to divulge the status of the probe.

John McNesby, president of the Fraternal Order of Police, continues to staunchly defend the officers. He is adamant that the officers did nothing wrong and will be back on the street soon. He wants the city to award the officers hundreds of thousands of dollars in lost overtime. In Philadelphia, cops can win back pay based on a hypothetical, arguing that they *would* have earned a certain amount of extra money had they not been placed on desk duty. In this case, the theoretical overtime owed to Jeff and the other officers could exceed $1 million.

George Bochetto, the bulldog attorney who defended Jeff and railed when we first met him, "What do you guys think you are going to do? Win a Pulitzer Prize?" still practices law in Philadelphia. About a month after winning the Pulitzer, Barbara and I bumped into him at a state awards banquet. He sheepishly congratulated us. He shook our hands while patting us on the back. He leaned in closer and in a half whisper, half mumble, said, "I didn't realize . . ." That moment was almost as satisfying as winning the Pulitzer. Not really, but you get the point.

Jose Duran, the bodega owner who captured the officers on video cutting surveillance camera wires in his store, lost his business shortly after the raid. He couldn't afford his mortgage and had to sell his large South Jersey colonial. He now rents a smaller rancher on a busy street. He works as a butcher in the meat department at a Costco.

Dagma Rodriguez and Lady Gonzalez struggle to get past what happened to them. They're angry and incensed that Tom Tolstoy remains an officer. "If it would have been any other citizen on the street, he would be in jail already," Lady said.

Tolstoy, who never met with or talked to us, does have a dream though: He plans to open a charter school for teenagers who want a career in law enforcement.

The feds stopped paying for Benny's housing. He had become too much of a handful. They wanted him to stay out of Philly, but he kept returning to the very streets where he had set up drug dealers. He felt compelled to apologize to them for what he had done. But that only made them more vengeful. Barbara spent more than an hour on the phone with one drug dealer, convincing him not to kill Benny. Eventually, we lost touch with Benny.

The hedge funds took control of the *Philadelphia Daily News* and *Philadelphia Inquirer* and got rid of the editors of both papers. A series of buyouts, budget cuts, pay cuts, and mandatory furloughs ensued. In 2011, the new overseers sold the iconic white tower that housed the papers. Morale plummeted.

Amid rumors that the hedge funds planned to close the *Daily News* and further slash the *Inquirer*, the papers were sold yet again in the spring of 2012—this time for $55 million, 11 percent of the $515 million Tierney's group had paid in 2006. It was the fourth time in six years that the papers had been flipped. The new owners were a group of local, high-profile businessmen, some of whom were entrenched in Democratic politics and fund-raising. They reinstalled Michael Days as editor of the *Daily News* and Bill Marimow as editor of the *Inquirer*. The owners promised to revive the papers, twenty-first-century style: online and behind paywalls. Time will tell.

Barbara and I continue to do investigative reporting for the *Daily News*.

AUTHOR'S NOTE

In May 2012, I landed my dream job covering the New York City Police Department for the *New York Times*. A little less than a year after I started working for the *Times* as Police Bureau Chief, my marriage to Karl fell apart. We separated in May 2013 and agreed to get divorced. With my personal life in turmoil, I decided to leave the *Times* and return to the Philadelphia area, where most of my family and friends are anchored. It was an extraordinarily difficult decision, but I felt that it was the right one for me and my boys. As Barbara often says, "Women really can have it all—just not at the same time." I returned to the *Philadelphia Daily News* in late July 2013 and reclaimed a desk, right next to Barbara.

—Wendy Ruderman

A CKNOWLEDGMENTS

This book, which grew out of our *Philadelphia Daily News* series, Tainted Justice, would not have been possible without the support of the entire newspaper staff. The victory of the Pulitzer was not ours alone. It was shared with reporters and photographers who fueled us with energy and inspiration as they filled the paper every day with breaking news, freeing us up to chase leads. Just as there are too many people to thank, there are too many adjectives to describe our colleagues, but a few that immediately come to mind are quirky, self-deprecating, tenacious, and all heart.

We're thankful to *Daily News* staffers, including Denise Gallo, Howard Gensler, Jon Snyder, Kevin Bevan, Pat McLoone, Michelle Bjork, Vince Kasper, David Lee Preston, Bob "Boop" Vetrone, Will Bunch, Michael Mercanti, and staff attorney Scott Baker, who went the extra mile to provide help and advice. Former *Daily News* owner Brian Tierney and *Daily News* editor Michael Days were fearless advocates of our work and champions of journalism and its power to expose wrongs and effect change.

From start to finish, city editor Gar Joseph made this book his baby. He selflessly read every word of draft after draft, infusing the manuscript with a brand of giddiness that was un-Gar-like.

We thank *Inquirer* editor Bill Marimow for helping Wendy parachute into the *Daily News* so she could dodge the 2007 *Inquirer* layoffs. After we won the Pulitzer, Bill, who cultivated a fierce competitive spirit between the *Daily News* and *Inquirer*, would always say "Savor it" every time we bumped into him.

To our agent, the ever-dogged Larry Weissman, and his wife, Sascha Alper—a talented editor in her own right—we thank you for believing in this book from the jump. You shepherded this project from the beginning, prodding us up each mountain, with unwavering zeal and commitment. You are a dynamic team. To the staff at HarperCollins, you had us from "hello." We're thankful to our editor, Claire Wachtel, for her seasoned advice and clarity, which greatly improved the manuscript and kept the narrative moving. We are indebted to associate editor Hannah Wood for keeping the trains running and pushing us to the finish line. Fabio Bertoni, assistant general counsel, has a keen legal mind and was a huge help. We are forever appreciative to HarperCollins publisher Jonathan Burnham and Tina Andreadis, senior vice president and director of publicity, for enthusiastically embracing this project and giving it life.

We're grateful to Philadelphia lawyers and court staffers who helped us obtain criminal files and other documents and lent their expertise: Jeremy Ibrahim, Stephen Patrizio, Bradley Bridge, Guy Sciolla, Ralph Silvestro, Theresa Costello, Marc Gaillard, and Joanne Franchini.

We'd be remiss if we didn't single out Philadelphia attorney and former Pennsylvania boxing commissioner George Bochetto, a ferocious advocate for his clients who graciously agreed to be interviewed for the book and patiently described the history of collectibles in his office.

Police Commissioner Charles H. Ramsey always told it to us straight, even when the truth was an ugly stain on the department. We thank our police sources in narcotics and internal affairs who provided us with invaluable information. We would name them individually but cannot because they helped us under the condition that we would not reveal their identities and therefore put their jobs and lives at risk. We're particularly grateful to the cop we call "Ray," who is not only a great officer and salt-of-the-earth person, but who also became a friend.

We thank Wellington Stubbs, former investigator at the Police Advisory Commission, for literally risking his job to cast a light on corrupt police officers and for sending Benny Martinez our way. We are grateful to Benny, who gave us the first glimmer into the lies, deceit, and secrets of an elite narcotics squad.

We're in awe of bodega owner Jose Duran and all the other merchants who entrusted us with their horrific and heartbreaking stories. If not for their courage, we believe that store owners across Philadelphia would continue to be victimized to this day.

The word admiration falls short to describe how we feel about the three women who spoke out about their dark encounters with Officer Tom Tolstoy. In doing so, they gave voice to victimized women everywhere. Two of the women, Lady Gonzalez and Dagma Rodriguez, not only allowed us to use their names and photographs, but bravely agreed to go on camera. This resulted in poignant videos rendered by pros—*Daily News* photographers David Maialetti and Sarah J. Glover. Even now, years later, the videos move us to tears.

We couldn't have gotten through the nail-biting angst of writing our first book without great friends. Those who read parts or all of our early drafts provided candid input, sometimes painfully so, but saved us from ourselves—they are Yvonne Latty, Dave Davies, Lisa Breslin, Cullen Murray-Kemp,

Harry Green, Nicole Weisensee Egan, Kristen Graham, and Stephanie Farr.

A few friends stand out for being staunch advocates of us and this book. Monica Yant Kinney became our honorary Slime Sista. Her enthusiasm for this book was infectious. Her feedback, along with that of her husband, David Kinney, was invaluable. Once, when we needed a quiet place to write, we camped at their dining room table, drank their coffee, and swiped their pens (though not ones on par with Barbara's favorite Paper Mate Profile ballpoints).

Hutch Raymer always had our backs. Practically a bodyguard, he looked out for Barbara after we received angry and, in some cases, threatening e-mails and phone calls from cops while writing the Tainted Justice series. While holed up in Barbara's house, tired and stressed from writing various drafts of this book, Hutch came to the rescue. This time he brought levity—baked chicken and vegetables and Southern Comfort instead of his 9mm Glock.

—Wendy and Barbara

The love and support of my family and friends is boundless. To my Slime Sista, Barbara Laker, I am so grateful that you came into my life. It might sound whacky but I believe my dad's spirit brought us together. You are a one-of-a-kind, rare friend; a talented journalist; and a darn good person with a big heart and a fiery passion for life. You bring out the best in me—always.

I thank my mom, Isabel Ruderman Amenta, and dad, Stan Ruderman, for giving me the lifetime gift of a magical childhood and building a solid foundation upon which to launch my dreams and embrace adventure. My dad, who died in 1997, was my biggest fan and instilled in me a love of the arts and a belief in myself. My mom is a geyser of energy and strength—traits that have rubbed off on me and my sister and brother. She taught us how to dust ourselves off and start anew when life delivers a setback, or a major blow, and the ability to delight in butterflies and colorful flowers. I'm thankful to my mom's husband, Alan Amenta, for his unconditional support and for being a loving grandfather to my kids.

I cherish my sister, Amy Ruderman Plassio, and brother, David Ruderman, for always being there for me, for rooting me on with genuine pride, and for bolstering my spirits whenever I feel low. I admire their capacity to see the bright side of everything. They inspire me to be a better person. I thank David's husband, Juilliard voice teacher Robert White, for making my family's life more musical.

My life would be empty—and far less interesting—without my boys, Brody and Sawyer. I never tire of their hugs or the funny things they do and say. They surprise me every day with their astute observations and wonderment. I thank them for indulging my inner kid. I feel pure happiness when I am alongside them building sand castles, jumping in piles of leaves, and sledding under a clear night sky. Brody and Sawyer, you have my heart, forever.

—Wendy

Even though, Seven, my rescue dog, can't read that I know of, I want to thank her for patiently waiting for dinner that came too late, and for her wet kisses and tail wags every time I came home.

The Tainted Justice series and this book would have never come to be without Wendy, my Slime Sista, the best reporter I've ever known. Some people come into your life at just the right time for all the right reasons. Wendy, you are that person. I look up to you like no other. You're not only my best friend, you're like family to me and always will be.

I am grateful to my cousin, Rachel Goldberg, who has been like a sister I never had. I want to thank my brother, David Laker, who has always been my cheerleader and believed in me more than I did. My dad, Peter Laker, a rare bird in the truest sense, could always make me laugh, even when I felt like crying. He taught me obstacles were just that—and I could climb over them. Thank you, Dad, for telling me I was special and could make a mark in this world. Those words put fire in my belly.

None of my life adventures—and there have been many—would feel the same or mean as much without my children, Josh and Anna. They have grown into kind and driven young people who I would like and admire even if they weren't mine. Josh and Anna—you inspire me like no one else. You have taught me to let the little stuff go and make the big stuff count. My mom taught me the power of love. You taught me that in the end, nothing else matters.

—Barbara

ABOUT THE AUTHORS

WENDY RUDERMAN has a master's degree from the Columbia University Graduate School of Journalism. Before joining the *Philadelphia Daily News* in 2007, she worked at several media outlets, including the *Philadelphia Inquirer*, WHYY-TV and WHYY-FM, the *Trenton Times*, the Associated Press, and the *Bergen Record*.

BARBARA LAKER graduated from the University of Missouri Journalism School and worked for several newspapers, including the *Atlanta Journal-Constitution*, the *Dallas Times Herald*, and the *Seattle Post-Intelligencer*. She began working at the *Philadelphia Daily News* in 1993 and has been a general assignment reporter, an assistant city editor, and an investigative reporter.